David Adam was born in Alnwick, Northumberland. He was Vicar of Danby on the North Yorkshire Moors for over 20 years, where he discovered the gift for writing prayers in the Celtic pattern. His first book of these, *The Edge of Glory*, achieved immediate popularity. He has since published several collections of prayers and meditations based on the Celtic tradition and the lives of the Celtic saints. His books have been translated into various languages, including Finnish and German, and have appeared in American editions. Many of his prayers have now been set to music. After 13 years as Vicar of Holy Island, where he had taken many retreats and regularly taught school groups on prayer, David moved to Waren Mill in Northumberland, from where he continues his work and writing.

OCCASIONS FOR ALLELUIA

David Adam

Illustrations by
Monica Capoferri

First published in Great Britain in 2012

Society for Promoting Christian Knowledge
36 Causton Street
London SW1P 4ST
www.spckpublishing.co.uk

British Library Cataloguing-in-Publication Data
A catalogue record for this book is available from the British Library

ISBN 978–0–281–06577–6
eBook ISBN 978–0–281–06578–3

Typeset by Graphicraft Limited, Hong Kong
First printed in Great Britain by Ashford Colour Press
Subsequently digitally printed in Great Britain

Produced on paper from sustainable forests

To Denise,
for keeping the eyes of my heart open

All things therefore are charged with love, are charged with God and if we know how to touch them give off sparks and take fire, yield drops and flow, and ring and tell of him.

(Gerard Manley Hopkins, from *The Sermons and Devotional Writings of Gerard Manley Hopkins*, ed. Christopher Devlin, SJ, Oxford University Press, 1959, p. 195)

Contents

———◆—————

Introduction

One Easter on Holy Island, a few things suddenly came together. During Lent I had been reading A. N. Wilson's novel, *A Bottle in the Smoke*, and I came across this passage describing the main character, Julian Ramsey, falling in love for the first time:

> Loving Anne transfigured existence, it changed everything. I found all bodily sensations were quickened by loving her . . . My appreciation of the way things looked was so profoundly enhanced that I felt in many respects that I had only begun to 'see' since knowing her. Colours were perceptibly brighter. Sometimes when I left her in the morning and cycled into Soho, I would find myself dismounting and staring with wonder at quite 'ordinary' sights, a tree, a bird on a window ledge, sunlight on a building which I had seen a thousand times but suddenly saw for the first time . . . I was not seeing a bird or a tree transformed into something else, but I was seeing trees and birds as if for the first time and seeing 'through' the eye, seeing into the life of things, so that the act of vision became a Vision, and a morning bike-ride an occasion for alleluias.
>
> (A. N. Wilson, *A Bottle in the Smoke*,
> Viking Penguin, 1990, pp. 108–9)

Julian discovered that loving changed everything. All his bodily sensations were quickened and he experienced a great awakening, a resurrection: it was truly an occasion for alleluias. He had entered into a new and brighter world where the ordinary had become extraordinary, for his eyes had been opened to look beyond himself. He beheld a world transfigured, a glory that was there all the time but that he had missed. Such a vision literally brought him to a standstill.

In this short passage there is a sequence that I find important to life. It is the ability to stop the busyness of our lives, to 'get off our bikes' and to have time to 'stand and stare'. It is important to our well-being to make space in our lives for the people and things that are around us at this moment, to be aware of what is. Giving our full, undivided attention often allows us to 'see' and know for the first time. We allow things to speak to us, to be subjects in their own right, with their own being, and we discover they have greater depth than we ever imagined. This seeing and knowing constitutes a giving of ourselves in love, a moving out of ourselves and our own preoccupations, and a receiving in return of love and a sense of joy in what we are doing. If we fail to stop and make room for the 'other', life can quickly become bleak and meaningless. Why should we settle for the ordinary when life can be extra-ordinary? With this awareness, this love, we will find many an occasion for alleluias and for rejoicing in the glory that is about us.

But the truth is that we often fail to see with any depth. We take a great deal for granted, including the wonder of our own being. We gain knowledge from books and computers but our understanding may not be rooted in actual experience. We can fail to see the extra-ordinaryness of the ordinary things we deal with every day, and if a sense of wonder goes out of our lives, we will find few occasions for saying 'Alleluia', or for praising or being aware of God. It would seem that the Church's teaching has not helped us to enjoy fullness of life in the world God has given us. There can be a gap between what we do in church and how we live outside, and we may need to discover how to be at home in this world, with God, and to know that God is at home with us. Our God can seem so transcendent that we fail to perceive his immanence, his presence, when really 'The Lord is here' and with us in our daily lives. We need to let him open our eyes and warm our hearts. We need to love and know we are loved: to enjoy life and to enjoy God.

The evening after I read the passage from *A Bottle in the Smoke* was Easter Eve. Along with a group of worshippers, I sat in Holy Island's cold, unlit church for about an hour, listening to the various prophecies. There seemed to be a lot of promises but we were still in the dark! Towards the end, in a reading from Ezekiel 37, came the question, 'Can these bones live?' What a challenge! I found myself asking, are we really alive or are we only existing? Are we open to all that is about us? Is the Church full of life or still waiting for the resurrection?

Soon afterwards, we went out into the night and began walking down a steep, rocky road, and I thought, how appropriate an image for our lives! We are so often in the dark, having a bumpy ride and feeling we are going downhill. But then we turned the corner and were met by a blazing fire. Its light reflected in our faces and our eyes as we stood there on the shore of Holy Island, on the threshold of a new day and a new world. We had arrived to celebrate newness of life and the resurrection of our Lord, who 'Just after daybreak . . . stood on the beach' (John 21.4). I moved towards the flames to light the Easter candle from the fire, raised it high and said, 'Alleluia, Christ is risen.' Everyone replied, 'He is risen indeed, Alleluia.' Then I prayed that we would 'let the Christ risen in glory scatter the darkness from our hearts and minds and from the world'. If only we would let it happen! If only we would: 'Let him easter in us, be a dayspring to the dimness of us' (Gerard Manley Hopkins, *The Wreck of the Deutschland*).

There were many occasions for alleluias after that, including the singing of the 'Celtic Alleluia' by Fintan O'Carroll before and after the reading of the Gospel.

The Easter fire, the candle-lighting and the alleluias impressed two young lads staying with us at the vicarage over Easter. We liked to have one or two young folk visit us during school holidays, as we lived in a beautiful place, had a good-sized house, and felt it only right to share these as much as possible. Brian and Jim were from the town and delighted in the wild life of Holy Island. They loved looking for birds along the shore and being free to wander as they liked. Though neither of them were churchgoers, they were willing to come and see what I did and to help. Brian felt privileged to carry the cross for Jesus, just like Simon of Cyrene, as we enacted the Stations of the Cross. The drama of the Easter ceremonies and the singing touched them both, and over the next few days Brian kept singing or humming the alleluias. Whenever he was enjoying himself, he found the tune or the words came back. When I told him that 'alleluia' meant 'praise God', he was quite impressed and said simply, 'Have I been praising for this lovely place?' I could only reply, 'Yes, I hope you have.' How I wanted this to be true praise to God for Brian's life in its fullness. Jim was much quieter, but before he left he said to me, 'You know I found Easter really exciting.' I hoped it had touched more than his emotions and would stay with him and affect his whole being.

The previous Easter, the Archdeacon of Lindisfarne had told the story of a child who went to church with her nanny, and of how this little girl, though not fully understanding the ceremonies, got caught up in the joyful acclamations of 'Alleluia'. On the way home she would suddenly exclaim 'Alleluia' at intervals, and over the next few days she continued to utter 'Alleluia' as an expression of joy and with a good deal of gusto. Nanny could not tolerate this for long and told her, 'You are not to say Alleluia. It's a vulgar thing to keep saying Alleluia and you must stop at once.' The child became silent and some of the joy went out of her countenance. How easy it is to undermine our delight in things with a few harsh words. There will always be people around who are afraid we are enjoying ourselves.

The week after the Easter ceremonies was full of the signs of spring. The sun shone, the hedgerows started to green up, flowers began appearing in the countryside and the birds sang to welcome the day. But one person I met felt grim. Tense and overwrought, he did not notice the sun shining or the beauty around him, and seemed to emanate a kind of darkness from his whole presence. Though well dressed and obviously well educated, he was in a poor state. I invited him to the vicarage and he told me his name was George. He could not look straight at me as he sat there but kept wringing his hands, and I soon became aware of his deep depression. He told me he was having medical treatment but did not like the fact that the tablets he was taking dulled his senses. He had a loving wife, a good home and a well-paid and important job. He lacked for nothing, yet an emptiness, a world-weariness, kept coming over him; though full of himself, he was unsatisfied. In the time we had together, before the tide closed in and the Island was cut off from the mainland, I could only offer a listening ear and an act of friendship. George made me realize that too often we do not see the world as it is, but as we are. We fail to let the glory that is about us touch us because we are uptight, preoccupied, un-relaxed and unable to rest. Sadly, I must admit I was glad when he was gone, and for comfort I turned to one of my favourite resurrection prayers by St Augustine of Hippo:

> All shall be Amen and Alleluia.
> We shall rest and we shall see.
> We shall see and we shall know.
> We shall know and we shall love.
> We shall love and we shall praise.
> Behold our end, which is no end.

I often use this prayer at funerals for it shows how, in God, our life does not end. I like the prayer too for the sequence it moves through. Much of the time we are so busy multi-tasking that there is no room in our lives for wonder, but in fact fullness of life is rooted in the ability to rest and the courage to let go and allow ourselves to attend to what is about us. The prayer has a lovely flowing movement, from resting to seeing, from seeing to knowing, from knowing to loving, from loving to praising. Augustine, obviously, did not think of rest as a time of idleness but rather as a time of harmony in our actions, when we cease to be out of sync with what is going on around us. Such resting in its turn will help us to see more clearly, and when our vision is clear we have a better chance of real relationships with our own being, our neighbours, the world around us, and with our God. When we love and are loved, propensities towards disintegration in our lives tend to disappear. Loving relationships lead us into joy and praise, and our relationship with God assures us of a joy that will last for ever. Death is not fatal for Augustine because it is not the end! The Christian's attitude to life is different from that of others because, in the words of Augustine, 'We are Easter people and Alleluia is our song.'

I would like to use 'All shall be Amen and Alleluia' as a basis for looking at how we should approach the world and life, and how we should come before our God. We will explore the natural ability to rest, see, know, love and enjoy, first in relation to the world around us, then in relation to our God. At the end of each chapter, a few simple exercises and prayers will offer opportunities to put these ideas into practice, and my hope is that by the end of the book we will feel assured that we are loved and that throughout our lives we may expect many opportunities for seeing, knowing, loving and enjoying: many occasions for alleluias.

Unbend the bow

Men go abroad to wonder
at the height of mountains,
at the huge waves of the sea,
at the long courses of rivers,
at the vast compass of the ocean,
at the circular motion of the stars;
and they pass by themselves without wondering.

(Augustine, *Confessions* X.8)

One day when I was still Vicar of Holy Island, a tourist opened the door of the church and asked: 'Is this Holy Island church?' When assured it was, he replied, 'Wonderful,' closed the door and left. He did not really enter the building or enjoy its special atmosphere, and I wondered what he had experienced, and if he had been enriched in any way at all. On another occasion, I was startled by the response of a young woman when I asked if she had been to Iona. 'Yes, I went there on a day trip,' she replied. 'I've been there, done that.' Neither of these people displayed much sensitivity to the beauty of the places they had visited. It was as if they were simply collecting locations, as others collect stamps or coins, in an attempt to fill the emptiness in their lives.

A friend made an interesting comment about his holiday: 'I'll be glad to get back to work and have a rest!' Too often our holidays fail to satisfy us because our inner being is disturbed: it is not at rest, so we do not find rest. Over two thousand years ago the poet Horace wrote:

> They change their clime, not their spirits, who rush across the sea. We strain at achieving nothing: we seek happiness in boats and carriage rides. What you seek is here, at Ulubrae, so long as peace of mind does not desert you.
>
> (Horace, 65–8 BC, *Epistles*, Book 1, 11)

We all need to be able to stop: to apply the brakes. It is foolish to keep driving around if we are not taking anything in. Too often in perpetual motion, we become blind to the beauty, the wonder and the mystery of life. Stillness and silence are what we need to foster awareness, and it is good to have times each day when we consciously pay attention to what is around us. The words of Van Gogh in a letter to his brother Theo are sound advice: 'Admire as much as you can; most people do not admire enough' (January 1874: *Letters of Vincent Van Gogh*, Penguin, 1997, p. 6).

When we admire something and give ourselves to it, we move out of the enclosed world of the ego and into a world of relationships and depth, where we have the opportunity to grow and to love. It is good to learn to welcome the gift of each new day. Start by noticing what is around you, the familiar things you may have taken for granted. Seek to be aware of all you encounter each day, especially the people you see regularly. Instead of straining ahead, learn to stop and enjoy what is happening at this moment, and be, right where you are.

There is an old folk tale from the Fenian cycle of Irish mythology, in which the Fianna-Finn are talking of music. 'What is the finest music in the world?' asked Fionn of his son, Oisin. 'The cuckoo calling from the tree that is highest in the hedge,' he answered. They went around the room, and each told what music they believed to be finest. One said the belling of a stag across the water, another the baying of a tuneful pack heard in the distance, and others believed the finest music to be the sound of a lark, the laughter of a girl, and the whisper of a loved one. 'They are good sounds all,' said Fionn. 'Tell us,' one of them asked him, 'what do you think?' 'The music of what happens,' said Fionn. 'That is the finest music in the world.'

To be aware of what is around us and 'what happens' to the world and to ourselves is a great gift, and one we can all develop. Otherwise, we may well miss out on the reality of life and be caught up in what does not bring us life or joy.

I used to think of myself as a bit of a toxophilite, a lover of archery. I owned a six-foot bow that was a gift from a friend. When it was not in use, I made sure it was not strung up tightly, because the longer a bow is left strung tightly, the greater the bend you have to make in it for it to be effective. This is done by tightening the bowstring even more, a process that, if continued, will bring either the bow or the string to breaking point. I've learned that life is very like that! If you do not relax you will get strung tighter and tighter, and a bow that is always bent will snap, as people who are always tense tend to do. 'Rest or snap' is a good warning to us all, and as we learn one of the great arts – to be relaxed and at rest in what we do – we will find that life goes on, and is indeed often enhanced, by stopping for a while. For through so doing, we will make room for new things to happen.

I would often take my bow with me when I was conducting a retreat, and show how in various modes it could be an image for how we react to life. If you look at a crowd, it is amazing how many are bent like a runner thrusting forward. Holding the bow with the bowstring away from me, I would say that this represents those of us straining towards the future, always planning ahead, imagining what might be. Such forward-looking prevents us from being in the here and now: our lives are full of agendas; our diaries are full of events; our inboxes are full of messages demanding an immediate response. In the story of *The Little Prince* there is a frightening description of someone who is too busy to give the Little Prince, or the world around him, his attention:

'I know a planet where there is a certain red-faced gentleman. He has never smelled a flower. He has never looked at a star. He has never loved anyone. He has never done anything in his life but add up figures. And all day he says over and over, just like you, "I am busy with matters of consequence!" And that makes him swell up with pride. But he is not a man – he is a mushroom!'
'A what?' 'A mushroom!'

(Antoine de Saint-Exupéry,
The Little Prince, Penguin, 1962, p. 31)

We may laugh at this in a nervous way, but how often could someone say to us: 'Where are you? For you're not here!' How well do we attend to the people we are with? Much of life can pass by unnoticed because our minds are preoccupied even in our leisure time, with computer games or television, and we are so glued to the screen or the set that we fail to make contact with the family and friends around us. By learning to stop, to let go, to relax, to rest, we will rediscover the freshness and the newness of the day. There will be time to notice the flowers, the trees, the stars . . .

Holding the bow the normal way, with the string towards me, the curve is now backwards. So many of us are unable to live in the present because the past vibrates so strongly in our lives. Perhaps there is a joyous event we find comfort in reliving, or a difficult incident that provokes guilt, fear or anger: we all carry many memories and some past hurts. Wallowing in nostalgia is often a sign that we are not at home in the present. We cannot live off Old Masters or past liturgies without bringing something of our present world and ourselves to them. The past and the future are very important, but we need to learn how to be *now*. The poet Rainer Maria Rilke, in his *Letters on Cézanne*, wrote: 'One lives so badly, because one always comes into the present distracted' (Jonathan Cape, 1988, p. 10).

When we are distracted it is hard to be fully attracted. So many of our modern communication devices help fill our moments without inviting us to be in contact with what is actually around us. Long before any of these inventions, Pascal wrote:

We do not rest satisfied with the present. We anticipate the future as too slow in coming, as if in order to hasten its course; or we recall the past, to stop its too rapid flight. So imprudent are we that we wander in the times which are not ours, and do not think of the only one which belongs to us; and so idle are we that we dream of those times which are no more, and thoughtlessly overlook that which alone exists. For the present is generally painful to us. We conceal it from our sight, because it troubles us; and if it be delightful to us, we regret to see it pass away. We try to sustain it by the future, and think of arranging matters which are not in our power, for a time which we have no certainty of reaching.

Let each one examine his thoughts, and he will find them all occupied with the past and the future. We scarcely ever think of the present; and if we think of it, it is only to take light from it to arrange the future. The present is never our end. The past and the present are our means; the future alone is our end. So we never live, but we hope to live; and, as we are always preparing to be happy, it is inevitable we should never be so.

(Blaise Pascal, *Pensées*, E. P. Dutton, 1958,
Thought 172, p. 55)

The bent bow is always tense and is often pulled one way or another, as are we. For the well-being of the bow it is necessary to loosen the bow string and allow the bow to be unbent, upright. Upright and uptight are two very different things. If the bow is always strung up it will not only become permanently bent, it will become distorted and weakened. Many people suffer from breakdown because of their inability to relax from the many tensions within and around them.

The unbent bow is not useless; it is in a state of rest but ready for action when need be. To unbend is not to switch off altogether but to disengage from what is distorting our lives and distracting us. The tense person, on the other hand, often detaches from people and things around him in an unhealthy way, as a means of protection. I am reminded of the words of Tacitus concerning the Roman army: 'Where they created a desert, they called it peace.' The stillness, the relaxation, we seek is not emptiness but a living in harmony with what is around us and what comes to us. To rest is not to escape from all that you want to do with your life. It is not to deny the many tasks and agendas that are yours. But it does give you the opportunity to live in tune with your surroundings and live in harmony with the people around you. And through cultivating stillness – which helps us be aware not only of each other but of ourselves, as unique living beings – we can begin to carry within us an inner calm that will be able to survive whatever upheavals we may face. Saul Bellow, the American novelist, said: 'Art has something to do with the achievement of stillness in the midst of chaos. A stillness which characterizes prayer, too, and the eye of a storm . . . an arrest of attention in the midst of distraction' (*Writers at Work*, 3rd series, ed. George Plimpton, Viking, 1976, p. 190).

The unbent bow is like someone who is all attention. Paying real attention to the world around us, to ourselves, to other people and things, is the way we grow in awareness and love. I know people on college courses whose minds are not really on what is being taught – sadly, attendance and attention are often two very different things! I felt like writing of one student, 'He was there but he did not attend.' To be attentive means to give of ourselves, to stop being self-centred and enter into a relationship of love. It is interesting that those who love what they attend to nearly always find it easier to learn and with a more lasting effect. This loving also helps to produce joy in our actions.

Whatever our spirituality, if we are to become what we were intended to be, we need to concern ourselves not with other worlds, but with this world that God has given to us.

It is here and now in this life that we need to deepen our awareness of what is around us. We need to be attentive to the place we are in and the people we meet. This includes being properly attentive to ourselves. We cannot love our neighbours as ourselves if we do not have a proper respect and love for our own being. In the same way, we cannot really say we are able to give our attention to God if we have failed to attend to the world and the people around us. I am convinced that those who do not listen carefully to others are not likely to listen with care to the word of God. We need to learn that the way to the Great Other is through other people and things. God speaks to us through his Creation. When we respect the otherness of people and creation, the holiness of life is revealed to us. The way to the holy is in the ordinary: the ordinary is far more extraordinary than we think or imagine. We can experience at any moment what Elizabeth Barrett Browning writes of in her poem *Aurora Leigh*:

> Earth's crammed with heaven,
> And every common bush afire with God:
> But only he who sees, takes off his shoes,
> The rest sit round it, and pluck blackberries,
> And daub their natural faces unaware
> More and more, from the first similitude.
>
> (Elizabeth Barrett Browning, *Aurora Leigh*,
> 1857, Book 7, lines 821–6)

The burning bush can be seen as a symbol of all creation, for the whole world is afire with the love and the presence of God. Suddenly you turn a corner and find you are approaching holy ground. The very earth on which you stand has the potential to reveal God's presence: each bush, tree, flower, bird or person has the power to open your eyes to the beyond in your midst. Like Jacob, if we are fortunate we will awake out of sleep and say, 'Surely the LORD is in this place – and I did not know it!' (see Genesis 28.10–17). We are all offered such experiences, though often our sensitivities are dulled and we walk by without noticing. We need to reawaken our senses and see the potential of each encounter, each person, each blade of grass, each bush, each tree, to reveal the glory of God. When the eyes of our hearts are opened in this way we will see a whole new world, and find we have occasions for alleluia.

The inspiration of the unbent bow came from one of the stories of the fourth-century Desert Fathers. There was a time in the wilderness when Abbot Anthony was enjoying the company of his brethren in a leisurely fashion. A hunter came upon them, saw that the brothers were not doing anything in particular and expressed his disapproval. He felt the brothers should always be at work, be at prayer or at least be serious. Abbot Anthony said to him, 'Place an arrow in your bow and shoot it.' The hunter did as he was asked. Anthony requested that he shoot another, and another and another. The hunter explained to him, 'If I bend my bow all the time it will break.' Abbot Anthony replied: 'It is the same with us. If we push ourselves beyond measure we will collapse. It is necessary, therefore, from time to time to relax our efforts.'

In seeking out the desert, the Desert Fathers were not running away from the world but removing themselves from a world that was not at rest. They were avoiding being caught up in a life of triviality that had no true purpose. The *quies*

(Latin), or 'rest', they sought was a desire to live in harmony with the world, each other and their Creator. True, they detached themselves from certain things, but that was to give them room to attach themselves to what mattered. In this way the desert helped to create people of great depth whose wisdom can still guide us today.

Stillness, rest, and living in harmony are essential to our well-being. Many people get 'burned-out' because they have not learned to stop, still mind and body, and be in tune with life around them. Let me tell you about someone who was forever on the run.

Jim was a good man and a hard worker. Very fit, he boasted he was available for work 24/7. When he rose at 5.45 a.m., he would check for messages on his mobile, listen to the news while he shaved, have a quick breakfast, then catch the train for his 60-minute commute to work. Of course, he got plenty done while travelling: he prided himself on his ability to multi-task. The pressure at work was intense and he rarely got home before 7 p.m.

Then one day, around noon, he suddenly snapped. After sitting at his desk for a couple of hours doing nothing, he told the person in charge he was going home and did not know when he would be back. He just walked out. Later, Jim told me that he felt he had run out of energy. It was as if he had been on automatic pilot for months: nothing seemed to have any meaning and there was no joy in life. He swung from being very uptight about this to being totally switched off.

Some people said that Jim was having a breakdown and suggested he go to see a psychiatrist. Others thought he should just pull himself together and get back to work. But I felt there was another dimension to the matter. Jim was not having a breakdown so much as a breakthrough. Something within told him that there was more to life than the way he had chosen to live, which was detrimental to his home life, his relationships and his health. He had the courage to stop and reassess things; the wisdom to brake rather than break. He described himself as like a Formula One driver, needing to know when to take his foot off the throttle, and when to make a pit-stop to prevent a blow-out. Jim was able to change the way he did things. He made more time for people, and for enjoying what was around him. Though he went back to his old job, he had a new attitude and worked fewer hours. Interestingly, he reckoned that because he was more relaxed, he actually achieved as much as he used to and got more joy out of doing it. It was well worth applying the brakes, to unbend the bow. We all need to make an art of learning to stop, relax, and live in tune with what is around us.

Many are drawn to Augustine because he struggled with life, spending many desperate years in search of peace and rest. By temperament he was passionate and sensual: he had a son with the woman who was his concubine for 14 years, and when he sent her away, he took a mistress. Augustine ploughed through books and philosophies, dabbled in astrology and tried various religious ideas, including becoming a Manichean and virtually renouncing Christianity. Yet he still felt lost, amid all his learning and sensuous living. He felt that his was a shallow existence and he could not live up to his own ideals. Yet his life would show that out of such failure, sin and ordinary humanity, beauty and truth could be found through God's love and grace. Gradually, while in Milan, he was attracted by the oratory of Bishop Ambrose. Here was no simplistic piety, but some of the highest levels of intellectual searching, with no hiding from the difficult questions of life. Augustine found much intellectual satisfaction, though he still had the nagging feeling that something was missing. He joined the catechumenate and was prepared for baptism on Easter Day in 386. Nonetheless, it was actually while he was sitting under a tree in his garden that his conversion came. Hearing a child's voice – or was it an angel's? – singing 'Pick up and read, pick up and read,' he grabbed his copy of the Scriptures, and the first passage that caught his attention was:

> let us live honourably as in the day, not in revelling and drunkenness, not in debauchery and licentiousness, not in quarrelling and jealousy. Instead, put on the Lord Jesus Christ, and make no provision for the flesh, to gratify its desires.   (Romans 13.13–14)

'In an instant,' Augustine says, 'as I came to the end of the sentence, it was as though the light of confidence flooded into my heart and all the darkness of doubt was dispelled' (*Confessions* VIII). After all his yearning and searching, Augustine found rest at last in God and in his Saviour Jesus Christ.

Exercises

Start the day with a deliberate act of awareness. Seek to be aware of what is around you. How often do you stop and give undivided attention to anyone you are with? Notice the world around you, including things you may hardly notice because of their familiarity. Spend a few moments rejoicing in the space around you. Celebrate the day and that you are alive. Rejoice in the gift of the new day and in all that is around you.

Learn from the unstrung bow. First tense up your muscles, curl up your toes until it feels painful, clench your fists as tight as possible, and screw up your face. Now you are tense! Let go and relax. Unclench your feet and hands. Stop your face being so tense. Check the rest of your body for points of tension. You have proved to yourself that you have the power to relax and you can help your body be more relaxed. Seek to breathe regularly and restfully.

Now still your mind with a single word or sentence. Seek to enjoy the presence of God as you would enjoy relaxing in the sunshine. This is the time to unstring the bow, to let go of all busyness and to be at peace. You may like to affirm slowly and thoughtfully the following sentences, leaving a gap of two or three breaths between each:

> The peace of the Lord is with me.
> The peace of the Lord is.
> The peace of the Lord.
> Peace.

Now rest and rejoice in that peace.

In this way, we find respite from the battles of life. It is only by learning to rest that we will have the energy to cope with what lies ahead, and it is good to learn to take many small rests during each day to recharge our batteries. They need only last seconds. In these moments, check your whole body for signs of tension, relax your hands and feet, your neck, your eyes and your face. Rest in the presence of God.

Let his peace, his love, his renewing powers flow into your life. Let go and let God work for you and in you. Unbend the bow.

Pray

I weave a silence on to my lips.
I weave a silence into my mind.
I weave a silence within my heart.
I close my ears to distractions.
I close my eyes to attractions.
I close my heart to temptations.
Calm me, O Lord, as you stilled the storm.
Still me, O Lord, keep me from harm.
Let all the tumult within me cease:
enfold me, Lord, in your peace.

(David Adam, *The Edge of Glory*, Triangle, 1985, p. 6)

Resting in God

The conversation of the brethren should help and cheer us, but God's voice speaks most often in silence.

Keep some part of every day free from all noise and the voices of men, for human distraction and the craving for it hinder the Divine Peace.

He who cannot keep silence is not contented with God.

(Society of the Sacred Mission,
Principles, SSM Press, 1930, IX)

While training for the priesthood at the Society of the Sacred Mission, I often felt besieged in lectures by words about God, theories of the atonement and the complexities of the Trinity. All this information was more than I could bear. Though I was sure it was good to know, it did not seem necessary to my relationship with God. At times I identified a little with Mrs Moore, in E. M. Forster's *A Passage to India*, when she was disturbed by the echo of the caves that turned all sounds to a monotonous 'boum': 'But suddenly, at the edge of her mind, religion appeared, poor little talkative Christianity . . . only amounted to boum' (Chapter 14).

I wanted to escape from words to the One who was being talked about: to get away from theories to the Source of all. The talk about God and his actions was often so abstract or cerebral that it needed the balance of knowing him and his love. I would wander alone in the grounds and fields, allowing the earth and earthly things to impinge on me, enjoying just being there, where a presence was waiting to be discovered, where the whisper of God was upon the wind and in the very air I breathed. I found the most fruitful time for me spiritually was when we were in the chapel in silence: there all the theorizing stopped and I could place myself quietly before my God. What God required of me most of all was my presence, my attention. What God seeks from all of us is not lots of words, or gifts, as much as a willingness to come before him: to abide with him, in him, and to be aware that he is in us. So often we fail to realize his presence and be enriched by it because we allow ourselves to be distracted by talking about it instead. For anyone preparing to speak of God, the act of being still before him is of primary importance. There is a great need for preachers who know God, who are filled by him and his love. St Bernard states this wonderfully:

> The man who is wise, therefore, will see his life as more like a reservoir than a canal. A canal spreads abroad water as it receives it, and a reservoir waits until it is filled before overflowing, and thus without loss to itself communicates its superabundant water . . . Today there are many in the Church who act like canals, the reservoirs are far too rare. So urgent is the charity of those through whom the streams of heavenly doctrine flow to us, that they want to pour it forth before they have been filled; they are more ready to speak than to listen, impatient to teach what they have not grasped, and full of presumption to govern others while they know not how to govern themselves.
>
> (St Bernard of Clairvaux, 1090–1153, extract from Sermon 18 on the Song of Songs)

Quite often when I sought silence I would find my mind crammed full of ideas and had difficulty settling contentedly in God's presence. I once shocked a small group of adults on Holy Island by saying, 'I live in a holy place: I have this beautiful church and surroundings. Early in the morning I come into church, and it is radiant with the sun shining through the east window. I kneel where St Aidan and St Cuthbert have knelt. Then, I think the wickedest thoughts of the week!' I went on to explain that this was because I was like any other human being, with a mind that wants to be forever on the move and easily wanders away from what it is actually doing. I received guidance on this wandering from two very different people with the name of Lawrence. The first was D. H. Lawrence, an author I enjoy as a writer and a poet. I sought to take to heart his poem 'Pax':

> All that matters is to be at one with the living God
> to be a creature in the house of the God of Life.
> Like a cat asleep on a chair
> at peace, in peace
> and at one with the master of the house, with the
> mistress,
> at home, at home in the house of the living,
> sleeping on the hearth, and yawning before the fire.
>
> Sleeping on the hearth of the living world,
> yawning at home before the fire of life,
> feeling the presence of the living God
> like a great reassurance,
> a deep calm in the heart,

a presence
as of a master sitting at the board
in his own and greater being,
in the house of life.

Above all distractions it is necessary to be at one with the living God, at home with him in our dwelling places and lives. We cannot create God's presence but we can rejoice in it and rest in it, though this is not as simple as it sounds! It actually requires much practice and dedication to learn to pay him proper attention. Yet there is a strange truth in the words 'Draw near to God and he will draw near to you.' In watching a cat make itself at home – curling up and getting itself comfortable in its owner's presence; purring while being stroked – I received an image of how we should rest in the love of God. I realized that God did not want a lot of words from me, he wanted me for myself. He wanted my undivided attention and for me to 'feel his presence'. Much later I would rejoice in these words by Iris Murdoch: 'Prayer is properly not petition, but an attention to God which is a form of love' (*The Sovereignty of Good*, Routledge and Kegan Paul, 1970, p. 55).

It is a great joy to be able to rest in and rejoice in the presence of God. We do not have to do anything but be there; the rest is God's gift to us. He invites us, as ever, with the words, 'Be still, and know that I am God!' (Psalm 46.10). Such silence and stillness is not emptiness, for in its depths is the space where God is ever present and waiting to be known. Of course, if we come to his presence feeling uptight about life, it will be very difficult to relax in his presence. It is by learning to be relaxed in our daily lives that we can learn to rest in God. And taking our rest in God into our daily life will bring an even deeper harmony to all that we do.

My other mentor was Brother Lawrence, who was born in the French region of Lorraine in 1691. While serving as a soldier in early adulthood, he suffered a wound that left him lame for the rest of his life. Lawrence spent some time as a footman, and then sought to be a hermit, but he found he needed a more structured religious life. So in middle age he became a lay brother within the Carmelite community in Paris. The next 30 years were spent working in the kitchen and as cellarer (the brother in charge of provisions). In time, his holiness and simple approach to spirituality became apparent, and many people – religious, clerical and lay – sought his help and asked him to teach his simple method of prayer. A little book containing a record of his conversations, letters and maxims was published, entitled *The Practice of the Presence of God*, which soon became a classic within the Church at large. It was one of the first books I used to help me in meditation and living, and has continued to influence me ever since. These words in particular have been a great guide:

Remember, I pray you, what I have often recommended to you, which is, to often think on God, by day, by night, in your business and even in your diversions. He is always near you and with you: leave Him not alone. You would think it rude to leave a friend alone who had come to visit you: why then must God be neglected? Do not then forget Him, think often of Him, adore him unceasingly, live and die with Him: this is the glorious employment of a Christian, in a word this is our profession; if we do not know it we must learn it.

> (Brother Lawrence, *The Practice of the Presence of God*, H. R. Allenson, 1906, p. 51)

God asks nothing of us more ardently than our attention: our outpouring of ourselves towards him. As God attends to us and loves us, he seeks our response. He does not ask for lots of words or ceremonies, but simply for us to give ourselves to him, to rest in him. Sometimes the use of set words or the outpouring of our own words may act as a barrier to God communicating with us. In any relationship silence and stillness are important, for it is only through these that we allow another person truly to enter into our life. Such stillness demands our attention in the way a birdwatcher in a hide is focused, watchful, expectant, and fully alert as he waits for a bird to appear. When the moment comes, he is ready and open to it: there is room in his life for this happening. The glimpse may be fleeting, but it is special and it is his, and the experience may stay with him for ever. Let us seek to rest in God in such watchful, expectant silence.

When I taught on prayer, I often used the word PACTS to illustrate a natural progression in our relationship with God: Pause in the Presence, Adore, Confess, Thank and Supplicate. I would suggest that the most important part is the beginning, the being still before God, and I often said that if we have ten minutes for prayer, we should spend at least half of it just resting in God and his love. I would have preferred to suggest nine minutes, but I felt this was asking too much of new learners. We need to Pause in the Presence:

to stop our overactivity, 'be still and know that I am God', focus upon his presence and open our lives to him in love. We cannot create God's presence – indeed we can hardly grasp it – but we can learn to rest and rejoice in it. The reality is that we are always in the presence of God, but we fail to realize it and be enriched by it because we do not make room for God in our lives. St Augustine expresses this in the most memorable way: 'You awaken this desire in us; for you have made us for yourself and our hearts are restless until they rest in you.'

In every life there is a space made for the eternal that nothing else can fill. We can surround ourselves with possessions and distract ourselves with activities while still being aware of an emptiness within. In fact, when someone declares they are bored, it often makes me glad because what they are really saying is, there is more to life than this, something is missing. 'Bored' can mean 'hollowed out', having a hole within us. Sadly, many people try to fill this emptiness by buying things they may not be able to afford, or seeking excitement of some sort, or indulging in food or drink or drugs. But this is like trying to quench our thirst with salt water, which only makes us thirstier than ever! The truth is that nothing can fill the space made for the eternal. A child deprived of the presence of a loved one will lose her well-being. She may be showered with presents and provided with every material need, but without a loving presence she will suffer from a great emptiness. Many who have been deprived of love in their early lives find it very hard to recover from this situation. They may have low self-esteem and a feeling of worthlessness. As St Paul wrote in his first letter to the

Corinthians, 'Without love I am nothing': we all need the love of others, and to live life to the full; we need to know that God loves us too. To deprive ourselves of an awareness of the presence and the love of God is to live with a hollowness that nothing will be able to fill.

Once again, Brother Lawrence is a good guide:

> One way to recall easily the mind in the time of prayer, and preserve it more in rest, is not to let it wander too far at other times. You should keep it strictly in the Presence of God, and being accustomed to think of him often from time to time, you will find it easy to keep your mind calm at the time of prayer, or at least recall it from its wanderings.
>
> (*The Practice of the Presence of God*, p. 47)

I was trying to teach a group of young people how important it is to learn to 'stop and stare'. If our days and minds are full then nothing really new can get into them. It is no use cramming our brains with information, or living vicariously through the lives of others (a great danger in contemporary life), and missing the experience of something for ourselves. I wanted the young folk I was with to appreciate the world around them, to see its beauty and be aware of its wonders. We explored how the precursor to any prayer or deep experience was the need to stop, pause and then to attend, to give ourselves to what was seeking our attention. We looked at these words:

> What is this life if, full of care,
> We have no time to stand and stare?
> (W. H. Davies, 1871–1940, 'Leisure')

As a group, we would start our time together by looking at something wonderful, such as light or rain. We used a standard prayer from the Celtic tradition that began: 'I believe, O God of all gods, you are the Creator of . . .'. And then the first person would add a single word, such as 'clouds'.

After this there would be a pause of about 30 seconds. Then the next person would repeat the sentence and offer another word, such as 'rain'. As we went round the group in turn, words like streams, rivers, pools, seas, dewdrops, fog, hail and snow were added. I liked to teach the group that the pause was as important as the words, as it let us be still and attend to what had been said. We ended the session, when everyone had contributed, with the words: 'I believe, O God of all gods, you are here and with us now.' We then spent at least two minutes in silence.

There was a hilarious side to this regular meeting because it almost involved me in a holy war, a fatwa! Many of the young folk were in the same study group at school and their meetings with me were monitored by a group of keen evangelical teachers. I think it would be fair to say that I was viewed with some suspicion because of my love for Celtic prayers and worldly things. The flashpoint came in a school RE lesson when a student was asked what I was teaching them at the moment and she replied, 'We are learning to levitate.' What a show-stopper! But while I like G. K. Chesterton's comment: 'Angels fly because they take themselves lightly,' and feel that there is far too much gravitas and not enough general levity in society these days, of course I was not teaching them to levitate: if only I could! The student had chosen the word 'levitate' when she really meant 'meditate' – learning to stop, to look and to listen, to stay and rest with one thing at a time: to be still before God.

Many forms of meditation say that you should relax completely but I do not believe this is possible. There are certain tensions that are necessary for life, and if our muscles totally relaxed, we would fall to the ground and become immobile. In the same way we cannot empty our minds. The mind is like a videotape that has recorded all that we have ever done, seen or encountered: all our life-building experiences are there, along with all that has been destructive or impoverishing. Much of the time we have a good degree of control over what we select from the video, but every now and then we find ourselves grappling with a random selection of past events. This is particularly likely to happen when we are inactive or trying to slow down. In the Far East the mind is often compared to a chattering monkey: as soon as we try to still it, it wants to race about. Like much of nature, the mind abhors a vacuum, and if we go on trying to empty it, it will not be long before we are dredging up silt and rubbish. Our time of meditation can be a fraught period when we find ourselves unable to concentrate, or thinking (as I found in Holy Island church) the worst thoughts of the day. In order to rest in God, we need to focus our minds on him. Every time your mind wanders, bring it back with a word or a sentence. I often use the following:

> You, Lord, are in this place:
> your presence fills it: your presence is peace.
> You, Lord, are in this place: your presence fills it.
> You, Lord, are in this place.
> You, Lord, are.
> You, Lord.

When your thoughts stray, return to him in love and simply say, 'You, Lord'.

You may prefer to use a single word, such as God, Jesus or Spirit, to draw you back. Repeat it with love every time something tries to fill the space you are opening in your life for God. Do not be put off by the struggles you have at the start: at least you are seeking to give yourself to him who gives himself to you. As often as you can, seek to rest in his presence and his peace: let the stillness be a part of you and of your daily life. There is always something impressive about someone who is calm amid the turmoil of life. It is a gift that comes by learning to be at rest in our surroundings, then with God and in God. Such restfulness is not optional but a duty and a joy; it is not idleness but a necessary openness to the beyond in our midst.

At church everything was about ready for Christmas. The wooden crib was in place awaiting the arrival of the Holy Family. Suddenly, disaster! As she unwrapped the wooden figures, perhaps in a little haste, the churchwarden dropped Joseph. I watched his descent, unable to do anything about it, and as he hit the ground, he shattered into many pieces and lay in fragments in the dust. There was sorrow and even a little pain expressed by the warden: 'I am sorry. He just fell from my grip.' I had visions of Mary as a single parent and Jesus without the protection of his 'father'. I wondered if a shepherd could stand in for Joseph but it did not seem right. The event made me realize that the disintegration of one member of a family affects everyone else and has repercussions in the larger community. We are all unique and cannot be replaced. Fortunately, things soon took a happier turn. The warden said, 'Don't look so worried. I'll take all the parts home and put them in the hands of a master – my husband's a dab hand at mending broken things.' As I watched her sweep the fragments of Joseph into the dustpan, I had my doubts. This was truly a case of 'dust you are and to dust you shall return'! But later in the day I could hardly believe my eyes when the warden called at the vicarage and produced a Joseph who seemed to have no cracks or breaks. He had rested in the Master's hands and been restored, made whole again. He looked fresh, having been given a subtle new coat of paint, but there was no doubt it was the same Joseph. When I looked at him later, by Mary's side, he seemed to shine a little. He became for me not only a symbol of the nativity but also of the resurrection and an occasion for alleluias.

At this time the other churchwarden was the local provisions merchant. His was a typical old village shop, which sold petrol and paraffin, wellington boots and engine oil as well as groceries and cosmetics. If there was something you wanted, he would strive to provide it, and he delivered around the area. He was open for business six days a week, and all the year round he was pulled one way and another with supply and delivery, with seeing to the shop and the outlying farms. Christmas saw him busier than ever, and he often did his rounds in perilous conditions, while always making time to help with the church's preparations. He had a wonderful description of himself at times like this, saying, 'I feel mosaic'; he meant not that his life was like that of Moses but rather that it was made up of little pieces and in danger of coming apart. As we worshipped on Christmas Day, you could see a man at peace as he rested in God. In fact this rest was often in evidence amid all his activity, for he loved what he did and was at harmony with his surroundings. For most of the time, he had an inner peace and drew those around him into it. For me, he portrayed what the at-one-ment is about, as he lived in a communion with the world and with his God.

Not long after that Christmas, I took the funeral service of a man whose life had slowly disintegrated. In his early years he had been an active person, but at some stage something had broken him. He became quite restless, wandering to and fro but never really going anywhere. As long as I knew him, he wore the same old black greatcoat, which got shabbier and dustier as he shambled around. I wondered if he even slept with the coat on, for he and it seemed inseparable. He refused most help but accepted the occasional meal from a kindly neighbour. One day she noticed that his curtains were closed at midday, which was not like him, and the local policeman was called. I arrived soon after and saw his old coat, empty and hanging by a nail on the door. He had gone and it had been left behind; but I felt that in the Master's hands, he would be restored and renewed and perhaps given a new coat too.

God's rest is about our being made whole again, with all that has been shattered repaired. Sadly, the Sabbath with its rules and regulations has at times seemed far removed from the idea of the rest of God. You cannot encourage people to rest simply through banning most activities, for rest is not merely the ceasing of activity – indeed, such a rest can be as empty as a desert – but being in tune. Rest is when you are not divided as a person and run by either the mind or the emotions alone, but at one with yourself and your God. It might be helpful to learn to repeat regularly through the day Augustine's phrase, 'God, you have made us for yourself, and our hearts are restless till they find their rest in you', each time placing ourselves in the Master's hands to be refreshed, renewed and restored. The calmness and peace that comes with this rest is beyond expression. It is a time of resurrection and an occasion for alleluia.

Exercises

Rest with God and in God. It is important to stop and let go of what you are doing. Give yourself a break from constant activity and justification by works. Let go, and let God have a chance to speak. Remember, God speaks most to those who can keep silent. Let the stopping not only be of words and actions, let it be a stilling of your heart, mind and body. Do a check over your body. Is it relaxed? Let go of all tension out of your hands, feet, neck and face; be still and at ease. Try and make sure you are comfortable. Now encourage your mind to relax; you may need a word or a sentence to help you do this.

Say quietly, 'Come, Lord God, in the stillness I am open to you.' Repeat it with each breath.

Breathe deeply . . . slowly . . . comfortably.

Reduce the words to, 'Come, Lord' and finally to 'Lord'.

Be still in his presence. Know that God is with you.

The reason for creating this space is not for knowledge, nor for peace, not even for love, but for God himself who comes to you. God is with you, so rest in his presence. Seek to be aware of the great mystery of God that is about you and within you. God will not force himself upon you. You need to open your life to him. Try and relax in his presence as you would in the sun on a lovely day.

Here are some words from Peter of Damascus that may help you be more at home with and aware of God:

> We must remember God at all times, in all places, in every occupation. If you are making something, you must call to mind the creator of all things; if you behold the light, do not forget him who gave it to you; if you see the heavens and the earth, the sea and all that is in them, glorify and marvel at their maker. When you put on your clothes, recall whose gift they are, and give thanks to him who in his providence takes thought for your life. In short, make every action an occasion for ascribing glory to God, and see you will be praying without ceasing: and in this way your souls will be always filled with rejoicing.
>
> (Quoted in Richard Harries, *Praying Around the Clock*, Mowbray, 1983, p. x)

Try to put the words above into action for at least a part of each day.

Pray

O Lord, you are with me.
Open my eyes to your presence.
Open my heart to your love.
Help me to make room for you
in my life, in my work and in my home:
that I may be at home with you
and know that you dwell with me.
In this space and stillness
make me aware of your presence.

31

The opening of the eyes

If the doors of the perception were cleansed everything would appear to man as it is, infinite. For man has closed himself up, till he sees all things through narrow chambers of his cavern . . . Unless the eye catches fire then God will not be seen.

(William Blake, 'A Memorable Fancy', *The Marriage of Heaven and Hell*, 1790–3)

I took a young relative up on to one of the great moors of Northumberland when the heather was in bloom and the bilberries were just waiting to be picked. We could hear the grouse calling to each other as we walked in the sunshine; clouds of pollen rose from the heather making the air smell of honey. In front of us was the wonderful panorama of golden harvest fields set against the Cheviot Hills. A buzzard wheeled quietly overhead. We stood in silence for a short time and then she turned to me and asked, 'What have you brought me here for? It's all green!' Poor lass, I had taken her out of her element – the comfort zone of shops and people – and she was only aware of the 'emptiness' of the countryside. We all need to stop in order to really see, but there is not much use stopping if we fail to open our eyes and our hearts to what is around us.

So often people seem unaware of our rich and colourful world. They enter a land abundant in history and mystery, a land awaiting our response, but if we cannot give ourselves to it, it will be unable to communicate with us. Remaining within our own agenda means rarely seeing anything new. I often think on the words of Marcel Proust: 'The real voyage of discovery consists not in seeking new landscapes but in having new eyes.'

It is only too easy to get life out of perspective, especially when we are tired or feel pressurized. I remember one day at the end of my first year at college, when I had come home and was among my old friends. It had not been an easy year for me, for the move from 'mine to monastery' was more than a culture shock, and I was really wondering about my future and what I should do. I had gone to church but felt disillusioned by the dullness of the service, failing to see that the fault was in me rather than in the worship. After lunch I made for my favourite place of escape, Hulne Park in Alnwick. It was a beautiful summer's day. I walked past Alnwick Abbey, along the river Aln, through glorious woods resonant with birdsong, and noticed almost nothing. I was unaware of the splendour of my surroundings. Reaching Hulne Abbey, which had once been a Carmelite monastery, I thought briefly of the Carmelites who made an impact on my life: Teresa of Avila, John of the Cross, who had struggled with the 'dark night', and my favourite, Brother Lawrence, whose writings had taught me to 'practise the presence of God'. But my perspective did not change much: I still had life out of focus. Sitting down, my back to the wall of the abbey, I looked out over the river below to the woods beyond. I closed my eyes. I knew by experience that wonder could not be far away in such a place. I reflected:

There is beauty all around me, and I am in the dark.
The sun is shining and the sky is blue, and I am
in the dark.
There is a bright world with creatures all around
me, and I am in the dark.

After a while I heard a rapping noise and recognized the working of a spotted woodpecker. I opened my eyes as if I had been asleep. A heron was alighting by the river; there was a deer in the distance. I had been so full of myself I had failed to see all this beauty. But now my eyes opened as if on a new, awesome world. The presence of God in his Creation was almost tangible: I had entered a sacred land. I sat rapt in wonder for a while, and all the way back, I thrilled at the privilege of walking in such a wonderful place. It was as if the person who had trudged to the abbey had been given new eyes – and a new perspective. Truly my awakening was an occasion for alleluia. I would later understand the artist Gauguin when he said, 'I close my eyes to see.'

Much of the time, we do not realize how wonderful and mysterious the world is. We go around with our eyes closed and our hearts untouched. We race from place to place in a way that suggests there is not likely to be anything much of interest on the journey. We expect instant results in most things, and life can begin to go by in a bit of a blur. John Ruskin could not have foreseen the speed with which we travel or are able to communicate with each other when he wrote:

There was always more
in the world
than man could see,

walked they ever so slowly;
they will see it no better
for going fast.

(John Ruskin, *Modern Painters*, vol. 3, 1856,
quoted in Mike Graves, *The Fully Alive Preacher*,
Westminster John Knox Press, 2006, p. 31)

I like the suggestion that 'to saunter' comes from *Sainte Terre*, the 'Holy Land'. Even in our most casual walks we are in the Holy Land, a land of wonder and mystery, richness and beauty, and taking our time may just help us to become aware of this. We need to learn to focus and give our attention and our very selves to what is before us. We are often offered the opportunity of new experiences but fail to realize their depth. Almost every day Denise and I walk for an hour or so in the country, often in silence to help us stay attentive to all that is around us. We walk the same paths regularly but are alert to the newness of each day. On 2 January 2012, we saw a flight of geese, a hare, a few fieldfares and a buzzard. We noticed the fresh tips on the willows, found a hazel nut that had been bored by a mouse, and saw that the hazel bushes themselves already had catkins. No doubt we will soon come across the first aconites or snowdrops, or something else that takes us quite by surprise. The important thing is that we approach these outings with our senses alert, ready to give ourselves in love to the new day. Each brings its own opportunities to offer thanks and praise for our own being, to share our love with what is around us, and to give glory to God. If you are able to open your heart and eyes to what is about you, even for a few minutes each day, you will find the world speaking back to you.

I will always be grateful that my father 'gave me eyes to see'. Though he was a wagon driver with many deadlines to meet, he would make sure I took in what was around me when I travelled with him. At an early age I was expected to know where roads went to, what interesting places we passed, and to recognize the birds and wild animals we saw. On our walks as a family, we took delight in spotting a wild hare, or rabbits, or a stoat, or various birds, or fish in the streams. We did not always have to name everything, but we needed to take time to enjoy what we saw. I lived in a world where there were adventures galore for those with eyes to see. I watched and shared in the miracle of life, in the colour and freshness of each day, with a sense of joy and belonging. I can remember looking into a sparrow's nest when I was about six or seven, gazing in wonder at the blueness of the eggs, and being over-awed by the thought that they too would bring forth life. Much later I grew to appreciate William Wordsworth's poem 'The Sparrow's Nest', which he wrote about his childhood:

> Behold, within the leafy shade,
> Those bright blue eggs together laid!
> On me the chance-discovered sight
> Gleamed like a vision of delight.

Wordsworth goes on to tell us how his sister Dorothy helped him become more sensitive to what was all around him:

> The Blessing of my later years
> Was with me when a boy:
> She gave me eyes, she gave me ears;
> And humble cares, and delicate fears;
> A heart, the fountain of sweet tears:
> And love, and thought, and joy.

We are fortunate if we have someone who has taught us to move out of ourselves and towards the wonderful world around us. The way we see things and people affects our attitudes to the world and to each other, and it is important that our vision is not impaired, or at least corrected when it is. I remember at one time having a small book with the title, *How to Improve your Vision without Glasses*. It was a system of daily exercises that had a great impact on me, with titles something like this:

> How to extend your vision and see further.
> How not to miss what is close to you and to
>   see more clearly.
> How to see what was once invisible to you.
> Do not miss out on the small things because
>   they are important.

Incidentally, it was about this time that I began to have trouble with my eyesight and decided I needed glasses, for I was not seeing things clearly at all!

In the Talmud there is a saying: 'You do not see things as they are but as you are.' Much of what we call spirituality relates to the view we have of ourselves, each other and the world, and these contribute to our perception of God. Vision involves not only eyesight, but all our senses. Seeing is not just looking: it is taking in, comprehending and, at its best, entering into harmony with that at which we gaze. As our consumer society constantly gobbles up one thing after another, making it hard for us to relish where we are or what is around us, we may need to work at re-sensitizing our vision and our senses. A time of withdrawal from too much activity can help us enter more deeply into life itself. Sometimes, by moving away for a while we can see more clearly on our return. This idea is expressed by the character Jen in the novel *Father* by Elizabeth von Arnim. James and Jen are absorbed by the beauty of the night. They have stopped talking and are watching the old yew tree and the stars, while listening to the cry of the owl.

> To Jen, who in her life had hardly known what silence was, it was a revelation. She listened, dissolved in a kind of awestruck joy. It seemed to her as if she were in the presence of perfect holiness, as if she were close to the very feet of God. She who had been trained irreligiously became, in this beauty, religious. She wanted to worship and fall down; she wanted to praise the Lord her Maker. And forgetting James, who anyhow was very easily forgotten, under her breath she murmured, 'And the Glory of the Lord was revealed' . . . James's heart gave a thump. That she should say what he often said to himself on similar occasions struck him as very wonderful.
>
> (*Father*, Elizabeth von Arnim, New York, 1931, quoted in Tony Hodgson, *Country People*, SHM Books, 2000, p. 261)

It is so easy for familiarity to breed contempt, or if not contempt then a kind of blindness. We are fortunate if something suddenly opens our eyes . . .

I remember when Bill came to visit us at the vicarage on Holy Island. Denise had taught him as a youngster and remembered him as being quite naughty and not keen to learn. Twelve years earlier, as a teenager, he had been obsessed by motorcycling. Now he was a fine young man. We took him on a little tour of the Island and during the walk he told us that he now was a regular worshipper at his local church. As we looked across to the Farne Islands he uttered, 'Awesome, how awesome.' These words were repeated again and again as he came face to face with the beauty of the place. He reminded me of how often I transpose the words, 'O worship the Lord in the beauty of holiness: let the whole earth stand in awe of him' (Psalm 96.9, BCP), to, 'O worship the Lord in the holiness of beauty: let the whole earth stand in awe of him.' It is often through looking at beauty that we are made aware of God and his holiness. I was grateful to Bill for opening my eyes wider to the loveliness around me, the awesomeness of where I lived. After Bill went home I wrote in my diary:

> Most people have become too familiar with the mysteries that are about them. They no longer see the beauty and the wonder of creation; they have ceased to thrill at the dawn or the blackbird's song. No longer do they stoop to enjoy the glory that is revealed in a flower or a butterfly, to discover the intricacy and splendour of a wing. It is amazing how so many adults fill their lives with triviality and worry over mere nothings when the glory of the world waits to speak to them. There is nothing free from mystery if you look deep enough or long enough. This mystery is almost the only way God can speak to us. If we close our eyes to the mysteries about us how can we hope to begin to perceive the great mystery of God? This great mystery is ever present in all that we call earthly or secular. If our eyes were opened

we would bow in awe before our Creator. Life takes place within the setting of a great miracle and we can derive endless delight from contemplation of it. Everything that is, is Holy. Once this is discovered, the whole world is filled with glory.

It is for this opening of our vision that the early Celts suggested we need to learn to tune and play the 'five-stringed harp' of the senses. Once our eyes are opened, the world is a place of wonder, mystery and great depth, where we meet the Other, who is always beyond our full comprehension. No longer content with living vicariously through books, television and computers, we will want to experience life fully by seeing and feeling for ourselves, facing the reality of what is around us, however strange and unfamiliar it might appear. Sometimes, by moving to a new place, we discover ways of seeing and experiencing, in depth that we have not known before. I have a friend who loves living on Holy Island but chooses to work in London for a spell every year. She cherishes the buzz of the city, and the opportunity to go to the theatres and the art galleries. She says that she would not like Holy Island half as much if she could not go to London, and by moving between the two, she keeps the places and herself in focus.

We often lose the ability to focus and contemplate because modern technology encourages us not to cherish the present moment but rather to aim at the next, and the next. In the busyness of our days, as we alternately appreciate and struggle to keep up with email, instant messaging, linking in, tweeting, we can lose contact with the very source of our being. The Roman philosopher Seneca wrote: 'To be everywhere is to be nowhere.' Are you here, in the now and aware of what is around you? Stop and see.

It may be helpful to think of the difference between sightseers, who are often more concerned with instant gratification than in fully taking in the places they view, and people like artists, poets and scientists, who give of themselves to their work, and invite us to look deeply at what is around us. I like the words of Van Gogh in a letter to his brother Theo: 'I want to paint men and women with a touch of the eternal, whose symbol was once the halo, which we seek to convey by the actual radiance and vibration of our colour' (3 September 1888: *Letters of Vincent Van Gogh*, Penguin, 1997, p. 394).

The idea that there is something of the eternal in the people around us should make us stop and look again: anyone viewed in depth will soon reveal just how extra-ordinary they are! It is hugely encouraging to know that, contrary to how we may feel, there is really very little that is ordinary in our world. However, holding on to this wonderful truth can be a great challenge. For this reason, I often read the opening lines of Wordsworth's 'Intimations of Immortality' with a little sadness:

> There was a time, when meadow, grove, and
>   stream,
> The earth, and every common sight,
> To me did seem
> Apparelled in celestial light,
> The glory and the freedom of a dream.
> It is not so now as it hath been of yore; –
> Turn wheresoe'er I may,

By night or day,
Things which I have seen I now can see no more.
(William Wordsworth, 'Intimations
of Immortality', 1807, stanza 1)

One of the great needs of the Western world is for people
who are seers – who have the gift of looking into the depths
and being in tune with the mysteries of life – to 'give us eyes
to see' what we are doing to the world around us, even if it
is painful to acknowledge that our way of life has to change.
At the time of writing, there is a drought covering much of
Africa, while the destruction of rainforests continues apace,
causing many rare creatures to become extinct and affecting
the world's climate. One of the major duties of our churches
and education system is to open people's eyes to the results
of their lifestyle. Can we see that the desecration of the earth
not only threatens our quality of life, but is an insult to our
Creator? True seeing demands an outpouring of ourselves
towards the object of our gaze, whatever the cost. Without
giving ourselves, we will never see our world clearly: instead
we will stifle our vision, our knowledge and our love. To live
life to the full, and to live in harmony with creation, demands
that we open our eyes. 'Where there is no vision, the people
perish' (Proverbs 29.18, KJV).

The idea of nature being a 'book' revealing God goes back
at least to the third century. When St Anthony was asked
how he managed without books, he responded, 'My book
is the nature of created things, and as often as I have mind
to read the words of God, they are at my hand.' A little over
a century later St Augustine would echo this idea. In one of
his sermons he said:

Some people, in order to discover God, read books. But there is a great book: the very appearance of created things. Look above you! Look below you! Note it. Read it. God, whom you want to discover, never wrote that book with ink. Instead He set before your eyes the things He had made. Can you ask for a louder voice than that? What, heaven and earth shout to you, 'God made me!'

Let the opening of your eyes each day be an occasion for alleluias.

Exercises

Learn to 'see' more clearly what is around you. Rest your eyes on something and give yourself to it. Each day of the week, focus on some created thing and look at it in depth; seek to give yourself to it and live in harmony with it. You might like to use the following guide, based on Genesis 1, to help in your exploration.

Monday: Explore the beginnings – the beginning of your life, the beginning of the day, the beginning of each encounter, the coming of light out of darkness.

Tuesday: Rejoice in the atmosphere, the sky, the clouds, the air we breathe. As you breathe in, give thanks for life.

Wednesday: As you wash, as you drink your morning cuppa, give thanks for life-giving water, for nothing would live on the planet without it. Discover the qualities of water, which are quite unique. Rejoice in streams and rivers, in rain and the renewing power of the water cycle that refreshes the waters upon the earth.

Thursday: Give thanks for the rising of the sun and the gift of the new day. Enjoy looking upon the multitudes of the stars. Explore the wonderful nature of the tides and seasons.

Friday: Rejoice in all living things. Choose a flower or a creature to focus on and look at it in depth: take your time with it and give yourself fully to it. Rejoice in the variety of life and in each thing's uniqueness.

Saturday: Enjoy your own being. Spend some time giving your undivided attention to someone. Seek to treat everyone with awe and respect.

Sunday: Make sure you are relaxed and rested. Spend some time in silence and stillness. Rejoice in the mystery that pervades all things and the presence of God.

Think over the following words and let them challenge how you see life:

> Do you have a sense of mystery? No generalization can be pressed too hard, but it does seem as if there is a thick sheet of glass placed, not between people of different creeds and cultures, but between those who have a sense of mystery (properly a religious sense) and those for whom wonder is a luxury we can do without. We can see each other through the glass, but we cannot hear each other for we are talking a different language, those with the capacity to see the extraordinary in the ordinary, and to acknowledge the mystery, and those who don't or won't.
>
> (Michael Mayne, *This Sunrise of Wonder*,
> Fount, 1995, p. 16)

Pray

Ponder on these words. Try to visualize each thing, then pray each line slowly:

Lord, purge our eyes to see
Within the seed a tree,
Within the glowing egg a bird,
Within the shroud a butterfly:
Till taught by such, we see
Beyond all creatures Thee.
      (Christina Rossetti, 1830–94)

Seeing with the eyes of the heart

'Good-bye,' said the fox. 'And now here is my secret,
a very simple secret: it is only with the heart that one
can see rightly; what is essential is invisible to the eye.'
The little prince repeated, so that he would be sure to
remember.

(Antoine de Saint-Exupéry, *The Little Prince*,
Penguin, 1962, p. 84)

One beautiful day by the sea stays in my memory. The
sky was blue and the air warm. A great number of people
were enjoying themselves, sunbathing or swimming, while
a little group played beach games. All seemed well with the
world. Next to me, a mother and father were absorbed in
reading, while their child sought to fill the moat surround-
ing her sandcastle. All she wanted was to have some water
around her castle. No one explained to her the impossibi-
lity of the task, and because of her great efforts, she was
becoming tired and frustrated. Suddenly, as yet another
bucket of water sank into the sand, her resources were
finally exhausted. Feeling as empty as her moat, she let out
a cry, 'Aaaaagh! Aaaaagh! Aaaaagh!' The sound disturbed
her mother, who threw down her book; her father could
no longer read his paper in peace, and frustration reached
deep into each of them. How I felt for this family, as the
daughter's feeling of emptiness eroded their well-being.
I have experienced this emptiness within myself more than

once and know it can be no more filled with things than a hole in the sand can be filled with water.

I know parents who shower gifts upon their children – expensive gadgets, mobile phones, MP3 players, televisions, designer label clothes – rather than spend any quality time with them. I even heard of one family who communicated by mobile phone from different rooms of the same house! We have to take care that family life is not dominated by a materialistic culture, with parents passing on unhelpful values to the next generation through goods and gizmos. Some families 'coexist' under the same roof, rather than share space and time together, with children in their 'media bedsits', surrounded by sound and communicating through the internet. Consumerism is one of the greatest causes of unrest in individuals and in society at large. Mechanical devices and things cannot replace personal contact. Families need to spend quality time with each other, to learn to give each other their love, and their undivided attention. Perhaps at least one meal in the day could be taken together, without the background interference of radio or television. We need each other's presence; we need to meet heart to heart. Healthy relationships within the home are the bedrock of any society. Relationships of mutual sharing, experiencing and responding are vital to healthy growth.

When I meet someone who has been provided with all their material needs and they say, 'Surely there is more to life than this!', I am delighted. Their heart is crying out for things of ultimate value, and this can indicate that they are open to discovering what life is really all about. We should encourage them to explore the possibility of letting go rather than stifling their dissatisfaction by acquiring yet more things or losing themselves in busyness, for these will not cure anything. Satisfaction in life can only be gained through love – knowing we are loved and being able to love in return.

Young folk often feel that they lack companionship, and if this is not addressed, they may suffer what in German is called *Angst*. Angst is more than anxiety: it is a feeling of great emptiness, a sort of heartache that is not easy to cure. Our inner being is like an expanding universe, and material things alone do not have the capacity to fill it. There is a sense in which we come from the eternal and we belong to the eternal, and our hearts need to be able to explore our great longings and seek to meet them. If we do not allow them to do this, we should not be surprised if we never really experience joy in what we are doing, for we will not have got to the heart of the matter.

> 'People where you live,' the little prince said, 'grow five thousand roses in one garden . . . yet they don't find what they're looking for . . .' 'They don't find it,' I answered. 'And yet what they're looking for could be found in a single rose, or a little water . . .' 'Of course,' I answered. And the little prince added, 'But eyes are blind. You have to look with the heart.'
>
> (Antoine de Saint-Exupéry,
> *The Little Prince*, pp. 91–2)

In the Bible there are more than 960 references to the heart. Interestingly, there is no single precise meaning: sometimes the heart refers to the emotions, at other times to the will, the memory, or the personality. More often it means our whole being. The distinction of mind as the seat of thinking and heart as the seat of feeling is alien to the Bible. Heart is the whole person, fully alive and ticking. When we say or sing, 'My heart is ready, O God, my heart is ready' (Psalm 57.8, *Common Worship: Daily Prayer*, Church House Publishing, 2005), we are saying that we are open to God with our whole being. Peter Toon writes:

> Standing before him in the heart suggests an attitude of sincere openness in the very centre of our being, the place where love creates love; further, the placing of the mind in the heart means there is no opposition between mind and heart, for both are open to God.
>
> (Peter Toon, *Meditating upon God's Word*,
> Darton, Longman and Todd, 1988, p. 95)

At the beginning of secondary school, one of our girls was finding things difficult. She sat near the back of the class and was often told off for not paying proper attention. As her written work began to deteriorate, Denise and I and her teachers all got quite concerned. Then we realized what the problem was: she needed glasses. She had not been able to see the writing on the blackboard clearly. We went to the optician, and were touched by my daughter's delight when she emerged, bespectacled, and found that she was able to read the notices in a shop window across the street. On the way home her excitement mounted and was quite infectious. She wanted us all to notice the grouse on the moors and the lapwings in the fields. Everything further than a few yards was pointed out to us with joy. Of course, we all need to be sure that we are seeing the world and people around us correctly. But true vision concerns the eyes of the heart.

Our inability to see the God in whom we live and move and have our being may have little to do with the weakness of our eyes. Abbot Nicholas, one of the Desert Fathers, said: 'It is a small advantage for the eyes to see if the heart is blind. The great world brims over with His glory, yet He may only dwell where a person chooses to give Him entrance' (quoted in Derek Webster, *Sands of Silence*, St Paul's Publications, 1993, p. 25).

Little by little, we can seek to pierce the veil that mists our vision; we can seek to see our God – who is never far off – in our daily lives and in the world about us. To allow God to enter our lives and our world is to expand them ad infinitum, and to be surrounded by a glory that cannot be fathomed but in which we can live and love and have our being.

For much of my life I have sought to be open to the wonder and mystery that is to be found in ordinary things and ordinary people. God is never far off: he seeks to speak and come to us through his Creation; often when people say that they will settle for reality, they have chosen to close their eyes and sold their birthright for a 'mess of pottage'. For there is always far more to life than we can see with our eyes: the divine radiates from matter and is ready to set our hearts ablaze. Behind every experience and encounter there is a beyond, a depth, a mystery. To cross the frontier into this larger world is to become a different person, a stranger in a strange land that is unpredictable and full of surprises.

> Just when we are safest, there's a sunset-touch,
> A fancy from a flower-bell, some one's death,
> A chorus-ending from Euripides, –
> And that's enough for fifty hopes and fears,

As old and new at once as nature's self,
To rap and knock and enter in our soul.
(Robert Browning, 'Bishop Blougram's
Apology', 1855, lines 182–7)

Almost the only way God can communicate with us is through the world and all that is in it. If we are insensitive to our surroundings, we will not be sensitive to God. The Desert Fathers, who had the needs and passions of all human beings, did not flee from the world but rather sought to escape the trivializing of life: they looked to live in a place where they could retain a sense of vision and purpose, where they could have a healthy outlook on all of life, where their hearts would not go cold. If asked why they had gone to the desert, they could have replied in these words of St Augustine: 'Our whole purpose is to restore health to the eye of the heart whereby God may be seen.'

The Church's task is to open eyes that are blind. The body and its senses are not only the basis of our vision, they are what keeps our vision alive. The senses help us stay in touch with a world that needs our attention, recognition and love, and we come to vision by being alive to and delighting in what is about us. Vision is fostered by love and not by thought alone. An important aid to keeping our eyes open and clear is a daily meditation: a time when we place ourselves before the wonders of the new day and the depth of what is about us. If we are frenetic and overwrought we will find it difficult to be attentive; we need to weave stillness into the start of our day, for as we begin, often we go on. The busier and more demanding the hours ahead will be, the greater the need for a stillness that will remain within us even through storms. It is in stillness that we open ourselves to God and give him space in our lives; it is in stillness that we learn harmony and how to live in tune with what is around us. Stillness opens the eyes of the heart to the greater world in which we live.

To see with the heart and into the heart of things is to discover a glory that cannot be captured on camera or fully recorded in words. This glory waits to be revealed to the eyes of the heart. It involves the bowing of our whole being before the wonder of another. Such seeing is always an adventure into the unknown, a pilgrimage to that which is holy, utterly other. We look with undivided attention and allow the other to absorb us until we are one with it and it is one with us. It is then that we come across

> objects recognised,
> In flashes, and with glory not their own.
> (William Wordsworth, *The Prelude*,
> Book V, lines 604–5)

What is given cannot be described, for it is beyond words in the same way that 'love', 'glory', 'holy' and 'God' are not really descriptions but indications of 'the beyond in our midst'. Time and again people have been fortunate enough to make this discovery for themselves.

When John Newton was saved during a storm, he believed that it was by the grace of God and this led him to change his life. He had been a gambler, forever chasing more possessions, but now he became someone aware of the depths of life, someone who knew that he was loved. In joyful recognition he wrote:

Amazing grace! How sweet the sound
That saved a wretch like me.
I once was lost, but now I'm found,
Was blind, but now I see.
(John Newton, 1725–1807)

Once the eyes of the heart are opened, we look upon the world in a different way. Beauty can be revealed by the smallest things. Gerard Manley Hopkins made this entry in his notebook on 18 May 1870:

> One day when the bluebells were in bloom I wrote the following. I do not think I have seen anything more beautiful than the bluebell I have been looking at. I know the beauty of our Lord by it.
> (*Gerard Manley Hopkins: Poems and Prose*,
> ed. W. H. Gardner, Penguin, 1974, p. 120).

For those with eyes to see, the glory of God is suddenly revealed through his Creation. On one occasion, when I lived on the North Yorkshire moors, I went out while the dew was still on the grass and the world had an early morning freshness, to cut some flowers for a decoration. I made for a group of peony roses. The very first flower seized my whole attention; it demanded that I notice it and I realized that I had never looked properly at a peony rose before. I had not noticed the many different reds and shapes of its petals, how velvety their touch, how firm its stem. What a strange centre it had! Little bits of information came flitting through my mind. I had read that the hidden root was used as a cure for palsy, and that the flower as a whole offered protection against storm and tempest. How did peonies come into being? Where did the first flower come from? I could have spent hours theorizing, but this flower was demanding my attention, presenting itself to me in all its beauty. I was enthralled by its mystery, which I saw as something to be enjoyed rather than as a problem to be solved. But more, under my very gaze a Presence had revealed himself in my little world, kept out before only by my inability to see him. I declared aloud, 'The Lord is in this place and I knew it not.' The peony had given me a glimpse of glory and I gave praise to the Creator of all. Later I discovered that the peony is called the 'Pfingstenrose', or 'Whitsun Rose', marking the time when the Spirit of God came upon the apostles.

If you look deep enough and long enough with the eyes of the heart you will find that all things are full of mystery and wonder. The wayside flower, the hidden nest of a bird, the autumn leaves, or the sun striking the roof tops: all have the power to reveal his grandeur. Adults, often too busy to notice and preoccupied with other things, can slowly become blind to the glories all around them. Children, on the other hand, are generally encouraged to be observant, and their curiosity and alertness to life make it easier for them to engage whole-heartedly with the wonders they encounter. It is possible to develop an alertness to the material universe merely for the purposes of gaining knowledge or for self-improvement, but if you believe in a world created by God, who loves you and seeks a relationship with you, everything you view has the potential of revealing this more clearly. The first attitude will keep you bound up with yourself and within the confines of human consciousness; the second opens you up to the mystery of the eternal in our midst, inviting you to draw near to God in love for what he has given you, to rest in him and to enjoy the mystery of his presence.

> A presence that disturbs me with the joy
> Of elevated thoughts: a sense sublime
> Of something far more deeply interfused,
> Whose dwelling is the light of setting suns,
> And the round ocean and the living air;
> And the blue sky, and in the mind of man;
> Emotion and a spirit that impels
> All thinking things, all objects, all thought
> And rolls through all things.
>
> (William Wordsworth, 'Lines composed
> a few miles above Tintern Abbey',
> 1798, lines 94–102)

Many is the time I have taken a group of young people on a walk to encourage them to see more deeply what is around them. If possible, they would each have a camera; failing that, simply a short cardboard tube. They were to find something to focus on, use the camera or tube to frame it, and look at nothing else. There was to be no attempt to capture what they saw on film or in words: as much as possible they were simply to give of themselves and their love to their subject. If they could look with their whole being, then the eyes of their heart would be opened and something special would happen – something they could not always put into words. Once we have seen a single pebble, a flower, a bird, and given it our full attention, we are growing in love. In giving of ourselves, the eyes of our heart are opened, and we begin to walk in a different world.

I regularly try to practise seeing with the eyes of the heart. Suddenly, with radiance, such love breaks through, like the sun breaking through the clouds.

> It was just like yesterday,
> same as the day before,
> the cat curled upon the mat,
> the milk bottle at the door,
>
> the robin comes for bread,
> I'd dropped upon the floor,
> then in a glimpsed moment
> it was all glory that I saw.
>
> I perceived it as it always is
> and evermore shall be,
> we are in the presence of God
> and live in eternity.

I pray also that the eyes of your heart may be enlightened (see Ephesians 1.18).

Concerning the heart, Augustine prayed:

Lord Jesus, our Saviour, let us come now to you:
Our hearts are cold: Lord, warm them with your
selfless love.
Our hearts are sinful: cleanse them with your
precious blood.
Our hearts are weak: strengthen them with your
joyous Spirit.
Our hearts are empty: fill them with your divine
presence.
Lord Jesus, our hearts are yours: possess them always
and only for yourself.

When the heart is warmed by what we see, when it is moved, or when we see deeply with the eyes of love – all these are occasions for alleluias.

Exercises

Choose a place where you can focus on one thing and give yourself to it. At first it is easier to choose something you find attractive and interesting.

Begin by being still and quiet. Make sure you are relaxed; let go of all tension, and all straying thoughts, as you seek to give your attention fully to the subject you have chosen: if you can, shut out all other objects. Using a camera, a telescope or a cardboard tube can help you to keep focused.

Look without analysis, without seeking to name or define, and let the other speak to you. Even if there is just silence, seek to give yourself fully to it, concentrating on it like you have never done before. There is no need to capture this experience in words. The important thing is the giving of yourself and the allowing of the object to be the subject of your attention.

In your prayer time, seek to give God the same undivided attention. Keep silent before him and offer him your love. Before you begin, think over these words:

God who made man that he might seek him – God whom we try to apprehend by the groping of our lives – that self same God is as pervasive and perceptible as the atmosphere in which we are bathed. He encompasses us on all sides, like the world itself. What prevents you, then, from enfolding him in your arms? Only one thing:

your inability to see him . . . The true God, the Christian God, will, under your gaze, invade the universe . . . He will penetrate it as a ray of light does a crystal . . . God truly waits for us in things, unless indeed he advances to meet us.

> (Pierre Teilhard de Chardin, *Le Milieu divin*,
> Collins Fontana, 1975, pp. 46–7)

Pray

Blessed are you, Lord God of all Creation, to you be praise and glory for ever.

As we rejoice in the gift of this day, open our eyes to the wonders and beauty all around us, and open our hearts in love to all that you have made.

Teach us to give ourselves to each other as you give yourself to us.

Blessed are you, Father, Son and Holy Spirit, one God for ever and ever. Amen.

Getting to know

God guard me from those thoughts men think
In the mind alone;
He that sings a lasting song
Thinks in a marrow-bone.
(W. B. Yeats, 1865–1931, 'A Prayer for Old Age')

There was a time in the eighteenth century when the London theatres were attracting great crowds, while the churches were quite poorly attended. The then Bishop of London asked the celebrated actor David Garrick why it was that actors who peddled mere fiction could draw and move the hearts of many people, while the most wonderful of realities seemed to be having hardly any impact. Garrick replied, 'It is because we represent fiction as a reality, and you represent reality as a fiction.'

The actor portrays his story with his voice, his hands, his eyes, his emotions and his whole being and so imbues it with meaning. Can this be said of all teachers or preachers? Knowledge is conveyed not by words alone but more often by how much we seem to be committed to or love our subject. So much harm can be done by dull presentation in school or within the church. The wonders and mysteries of this world are never dull – and nor is life itself – but they can be dully represented. I remember teachers and worship leaders who inspired me because they loved what they were doing and were passionate to communicate this. I am also aware that I was put off reading certain authors through teaching that seemed to put knowing facts for exams above being inspired by an actual book. Critical analysis alone can kill the thrill of the story: it reminds me of dissecting frogs at school, and feeling that what I had in front of me sadly lacked the thrill of watching a frog jump, or hearing it croak in the pond, or seeing a whole colony of them together at spawning time.

Often when I am listening to a lecture that seems dull, the poem 'A Prayer for Old Age' by Yeats comes to mind. Good teaching is not just the conveying of facts but also the nurturing of love for what is being taught. Thinking is not restricted to the mind; the person who is able to think deeply does so with their whole being – as Yeats would say, 'in the marrow-bone'. Bone marrow is responsible for creating red blood cells, platelets and white blood cells – approximately 500 billion per day in all – and can be viewed as the very source of life. For Yeats, thinking 'in the marrow-bone' reflects living life in all its fullness. It is holistic, involving not only facts but also reality and our relation to it. Facts alone do not translate into real knowledge: facts can be written down and memorized, but what we know with our whole being cannot. I have a friend who hardly ever reads a book or goes to the theatre; he scans reviews and précis to get information. He can tell you the names of characters and give you a summary of a plot but his heart has not been stirred, nor has he been angered or irritated by a novel or a play. He is not even interested in using the facts he hoards to shine at quizzes! He only wants contact with the bare bones, not the full body. I am reminded of some words in a play by Christopher Fry:

Facts? Bones, Colonel. The skeleton
I've seen dangling in the School of Anatomy
Is made of facts. But any one of the students
Makes the skeleton look like a perfect stranger.
(Christopher Fry, *The Dark is Light Enough*,
Act 2, in *Collected Plays*,
Oxford University Press, 1971)

An experience from my school days will tell you much about my attitude towards learning and knowledge. It revolves around a comment made to my mother by the headmaster at my junior school, Mr Elliott. He was aware that life was far from simple for me and had taken an interest in some of my struggles with learning. One day when he was teaching us fractions, which I enjoyed and found quite easy, something else caught my attention. I was sitting near the window and heard a blackbird outside singing a wonderful song. Each note delighted and held me and it would be fair to say that my attention was not on the blackboard or the lesson. Enraptured, I suddenly heard a voice demanding, 'David Adam, do the next one.' I did not know what the 'next one' was and remained silent. Understanding, and without comment, Mr Elliott pointed to the one in question and I was able to answer it without a problem. Later in the day, when he was telling my mother about some coming event, he added in a kindly voice, 'I think David is more interested in the blackbird than the blackboard.' I might have forgotten this incident were it not for the complexities of language. My mother later conveyed it to my father in her native tongue, Northumbrian, remarking, 'Mr Elliott says David is more interested in the blackbord than the blackbord.' My father could not understand what this was about at all until my mother explained.

I still have a fear of being full of book knowledge, of abstract knowledge, but at the same time being out of touch with life. The much parodied absent-minded professor or mad scientist know their stuff, but not what really makes the world tick. There is always a danger we will simply speculate about living rather than risk the adventure of actually doing so; that we will gain the knowledge but fail to have the experience. As we saw before, knowing about is very different from knowing personally.

I like studying maps, tracing river valleys, looking at contours and the shape of land. I can recite the heights of mountains and the courses of rivers, but that does not give me much impression of what they are like in reality. A dimension, if not many dimensions, are missing. How can a map convey the grandeur and scale of walking in an Austrian valley in the spring sunshine? Or the romance of being ferried around Venice on a moonlit night in a gondola? In a sense, such experiences take us to a totally different world. By being there we open ourselves to reality, and enter into a personal relationship with a particular place. No book or film can offer us such a personal encounter, though they can help us to enjoy what we have seen and felt even more. There is no alternative to actually being in a place, giving it our attention and our love.

Yet there are people who visit the Austrian Alps or Venice who are hardly touched by the glories around them. They collect postcards and take photographs, but remain uninspired: what is seen with the eyes does not enter the heart. It is just another place. This is often the experience of the tourist who looks at too much too quickly, seeking to capture images but not really engaging with what they are photographing. Sometimes it is necessary to put the camera aside, to look with the eyes of the heart, and truly give ourselves to the glory we are being offered. To those who come with the eyes of the heart open, ready to give their attention and themselves, there are new experiences to enjoy every day and new things around every corner to know and love.

When I was training for the ministry I had to study New Testament Greek. I was never very good at it, for somehow I could not get the feel of it as a 'living' language. My tutor once told me, 'You are not learning Greek very well for you do not love it enough. We are not a cramming school; you are here to learn to love what you are taught.' I was looking on Greek as an object to master, to possess. But it gradually dawned on me that we do not have *objects* to study in education but *subjects*, and we will not progress well until we discover that a subject has a life of its own, until we give it our attention and begin to love it. We all learn subjects we are fond of far more easily and quickly than those we do not. Though I never became a Greek scholar, from that moment I began to see how its words had depth and were seeking to convey reality.

Gustav Doré was a French book illustrator and artist of the mid nineteenth century whose work included 238 woodcuts, illustrating a wide variety of biblical stories. Editions of the Bible containing his illustrations were so popular they ran to nearly 1,000 in all. One day, Doré was approached by a young artist who sought his comments on a painting he had done of Jesus. Doré looked it for a long time before replying. When he did it was in one sentence: 'You do not love him enough, or you would paint him better.'

There are many who can tell you the story of Jesus but have not been touched by it. The sad thing is that this is often true of students of religious education, who have learned the facts of Christianity (or Judaism, Islam or another faith) from people who have never experienced its height and depth and are not committed to it. They can give you the bare bones of Jesus' life but they cannot explain the resurrection experience. They may know a lot *about* Jesus but they do not *know* him personally: their knowledge is hearsay and in the past tense. We need people who can tell us of the risen Lord – who is here and with us now – and whose hearts are on fire with love for him. The 'facts alone' approach is not taken only by non-believers: there are those who study theology but do not pray regularly or enjoy the presence of God; there are those who can discuss the atonement but have no awareness of being at one with God. If knowledge is in the mind alone, people will often communicate the facts in a dull manner. There is a big gap between saying we believe and saying we know: while the creed can be learned, the presence and power of God have to be experienced, and we need people who can pass on knowledge with passion, awe, reverence and joy. Only the person who lives a certain kind of life can truly talk of God with fire in their hearts and glowing eyes.

There is a story about a church that was visited by two preachers. The first was a great Hebrew scholar who was well known for his research into the meaning of words. The second was a lay preacher who spent most of his time working on a farm. The Sunday they came, they were both invited to preach on the good Shepherd and the twenty-third Psalm. The scholar preached in the morning, the lay preacher in the evening. Afterwards one of the congregation remarked how good both men were at speaking, but while the scholar knew the meanings of the Psalm, he felt the lay preacher knew and loved the Shepherd.

At the beginning of 2012, I attended the North Northumberland Bird Club, which meets in the small community of Bamburgh. On this occasion, the room was packed with about 100 people who had gathered to listen to an award-winning Scottish photographer and look at his PowerPoint presentation on 'Birds, Birds, Birds'. His enthusiasm, love for and dedication to his subject came across time and time again through stories such as how he spent 11 hours overnight in a small cramped hide to see and photograph the blackcocks lekking.* One award-winning photograph showed some grouse, and he explained that he had not managed to get many photographs on that occasion because the birds were stressed by the winter, and he did not want to upset them any further. He emphasized that he was a bird photographer and not a photographer of birds: birds were far more important to him than getting the perfect shot. Though he wanted to know as much as possible about birds and capture them on camera, he sought to do this without disturbing them in any way. His knowledge as well as his talent came across clearly. Above all, he revealed a deep love for his subject.

---

* A lek is a gathering of male blackcocks for the purposes of competitive mating display. Leks assemble before and during the breeding season on a regular basis.

True knowledge involves our whole being in a living relationship. Thinking we know something can prevent us from experiencing the real thing, from being aware of what is confronting us in the now. Imposed ideas and views from people who are not thrilled by them are as dangerous in the education system as in the Church. We often hear people talk of deep things but with little depth. The difficulty is that you cannot write depth into the curriculum. Teaching on the horizontal plane involves ideas, memories, past encounters and a great collection of facts. But true knowledge also requires the vertical: the now and the uniqueness of what is before us; that which cannot be classified or pressed into ideas or words; the possibility of encounter with the other in all its mystery. On the horizontal plane we can talk of knowing, but on the vertical plane we enter a world that refuses to be defined only in concepts. On the horizontal plane we can talk of things, objects, as if we possess them: on the vertical plane we have a relationship with subjects who have a being of their own. A healthy person lives on both planes. We all need to acquire information, and this process often leads us into the depth of our own experience. In our getting to know, we must realize that so much of life is lost if pressed into dry mental constructions alone: we must never confuse thinking about something for the real thing. Reality is always full of wonder and newness. As I've mentioned, D. H. Lawrence was an author whose writings have helped me to enjoy the world around me, and I often think on these words of his:

Now the great and fatal fruit of our civilisation, which is a civilisation based on knowledge, and hostile to experience, is boredom. All our wonderful education and learning is producing a grand sum total of boredom. They are bored because they experience nothing. And they experience nothing because the wonder has gone out of them. And when wonder has gone out of a man he is dead. He is henceforth only an insect. When all comes to all, the most precious element in this life is wonder.

> (*D. H. Lawrence: Selected Literary Criticism*,
> ed. A. Beal, Viking, 1982, pp. 7–8)

Wonder is an essential element in all true learning, for wonder acknowledges that there is always a beyond in our midst. Wonder keeps us aware that the knowledge we have of people, of places, of music, of art, of literature, cannot be affirmed with absolute certainty, for there is always more to it, an otherness that we cannot fully sum up. If we lose contact with life as a mystery, we begin to lose contact with life itself. When we lose wonder we begin to look at life as a problem to be solved rather than as a mystery to be enjoyed. Closed-circuit dogmatism threatens to deaden our sensitivity to what is, to the new and to the challenging. We can protect a past stance at the expense of ignoring or denying the present and the future. We often avoid reality because we do not want to acknowledge that life is forever changing, and for this reason we cannot hold the otherness of people and places in our mind with any fixedness. We have to be able to respond to the now and the new, yet often our set concepts will not allow us to do this. We need to learn that true knowledge grows and changes and is not as predictable as we tend to imagine.

Once I was contacted by a bishop's chaplain, who said that the bishop wanted to know if I would come and speak on 'Who was Jesus?' I asked him if a talk on a historic person was required, for if so I would set it 2,000 years ago. Did the bishop really want me to talk on 'Who was Jesus?' There was a pause and a rustling of papers, and then the chaplain replied, 'I am sorry, it does say, "Who is Jesus?".' By now I was sensing an interesting diversion, and said, 'I have lived with the same woman for over 25 years and I still do not understand her! I can hardly say I know who she is; I hardly understand myself! How can I say who Jesus is?' Poor chaplain, little did he know this was a favourite theme of mine. However, I shortened his torment by telling him I would attempt to say something.

If our approach to life is open and aware, we will soon discover that each human being has an elusiveness that is unique to them and that we can only experience in part. At all times we have to be sensitive to their otherness. We cannot press who they are into pages or pin them down as we would a butterfly, for that would destroy them. For about 20 years, I carried around in my Bible some pansies that were pressed from a beautiful garden. They reminded me of a place I loved and once called home, but they encouraged me to write this:

> Pressed flowers are like words
> longing for an experience lost:
> seeking to retain what has been
> unable to be captured between pages.
> We can still touch them.
> But where is the coolness of the stem

and the heavy scent of summer,
the joy of them dancing in the breeze?

Words cannot capture experience:
life cannot be pressed into pages:
words cannot hold the Almighty Word,
God made flesh and living among us.
Pressed flowers are like words,
living flowers are an experience.

(David Adam, *A Celebration of
Summer*, SPCK, 2006)

There is always more than we can ever see or know; there
is movement, depth and life that cannot be tied down in
fixed concepts. Each person and each thing is full of mystery
for us to enjoy. It is for this reason I like these words of
D. H. Lawrence:

Now I absolutely flatly deny that I am a soul, or a body,
or a mind, or an intelligence, or a brain, or a nervous
system, or a bunch of glands, or any of the bits of the
rest of me. The whole is greater than the parts. And
therefore I am a man alive, am greater than my soul,
or spirit, or body, or mind or consciousness, or anything
that is merely part of me. I am a man alive and as long
as I can, I intend to go on being man alive.

('Why the novel matters', *D. H. Lawrence: Selected
Literary Criticism*, ed. A. Beal, Viking, 1982, p. 105)

In the same essay Lawrence describes the Bible as 'about
man alive ... Man alive not mere bits,' and he continues
by saying, 'What we mean by living is, of course, just as

indescribable as what we mean by *being*' (p. 107). Such thoughts can be traced back to the Early Fathers of the Church. Irenaeus in the second century said: 'The glory of God is man alive: and the life of man is the vision of God.' The way we live shows what we believe, and if we lack vitality through our own idleness we do not live up to what God has called us to be. God is concerned with our whole mysterious being. Deep calls to deep, and it is when we begin to realize that our being has great depth that life becomes an adventure. I agree wholeheartedly with John V. Taylor when he says, in *The Go-Between God*: 'I believe there is nothing more needed by humanity today . . . than the recovery of a sense of "beyondness" in the whole of life to revive the springs of wonder and adoration' (SCM Press, 1972, p. 45).

This in its turn reminds me of Jesus' saying that 'one's life does not consist in the abundance of possessions' (Luke 12.15). It is possible to get into the way of regarding our concept of another person as something we possess, but our ideas about someone are not the person: life defies definition and we can never fully know another. There is always a beyond in our midst, a uniqueness that we ought to approach with reverence and awe. All of life is a mystery but we often avoid this truth because it disturbs us – it is more comforting to think of life as packaged, caged and comprehensible. Our education system and churches ought to seek to free us from this kind of restrictive thinking so that we can live adventurously, discovering afresh each day the extraordinary in the ordinary. The world of the other always transcends our own; the great Other, who is God, is contained in the mystery of being.

Never believe that the world or humankind has lost its glory. If we follow the crowds and fill our lives with noise and busyness, we may never see, hear or be aware of the wonder around us, but nonetheless, it waits to be revealed. We simply need to reawaken our senses in order to seek and meet God through this world, in which the so-called ordinary has the capacity to become extraordinary, in which nothing is truly secular, for all is holy. Our knowledge of each other and of the world around us is bound up with our awareness of the mystery of Creation and its Creator: 'Ever since the creation of the world his eternal power and divine nature, invisible though they are, have been understood and seen through the things he has made' (Romans 1.20).

Bill, Denise's pupil from Danby who found Holy Island so 'awesome', made me realize how easy it is to become over-familiar with our surroundings and to miss the wonder and mystery that is all around us. In the pressures of life, we fail to see the simple beauty of a flower or a bird. But if the eyes of the heart are opened, we will be full of awe at the world and its Creator, which we can experience at any moment. As Gerard Manley Hopkins writes in his poem 'God's Grandeur':

> The world is charged with the grandeur of God.
> It will flame out, like shining from shook foil;
> It gathers to a greatness, like the ooze of oil
> Crushed. Why do men then now not reck his rod?
> Generations have trod, have trod, have trod;
> And all is seared with trade; bleared, smeared
>   with toil;

And wears man's smudge and shares man's smell:
  the soil
Is bare now, nor can foot feel, being shod.

And for all this, nature is never spent;
There lives the dearest freshness deep down things.
     (*Gerard Manley Hopkins: Poems and Prose*,
       ed. W. H. Gardner, Penguin, 1974, p. 27)

The joy of living is to discover, or rediscover, the 'deep down freshness in things', to be in touch with the other and so be open to the great Other who is God. To do this we need to be able to give ourselves in love. In one of his sermons St Augustine said: 'Put love in all things you do and they will make sense. Take love away and they become worthless and empty.' When knowledge and love go together, our whole being is transfigured by what we learn; such a transfiguration is always an occasion for alleluias.

Exercises

Give thanks for your loved ones and their mystery. Acknowledge that we should never take each other for granted. Each day we can discover new depths in people. Rejoice that there is always more to them than you know.

There is a sense in which we are all new every morning.

Think on these words:

All around us, to right and left, in front and behind, above and below, we have only to go a little beyond the frontier of sensible appearances in order to see the divine welling up and showing through . . . by means of all created things without exception, the divine assails us, penetrates us, moulds us. We imagined it as distant and inaccessible, whereas in fact we live steeped in its burning layers. *In eo vivimus.* As Jacob said, awakening from his dream, the world, this palpable world, which we were wont to treat with the boredom and disrespect with which we habitually regard places with no sacred association for us, is in truth a holy place, and we did not know it. *Venite adoremus.*

(Pierre Teilhard de Chardin, *Le Milieu divin*,
Collins Fontana, 1975, p. 112)

Pray

Disturb us, Lord, when we are too well pleased with ourselves, when our dreams have come true because we have dreamed too little, when we have arrived safely because we sailed too close to the shore.

Disturb us, Lord, when, with the abundance of things we possess, we have lost our thirst for the waters of life; having fallen in love with life, we have ceased to dream of eternity and in our efforts to build a new earth, we have allowed our vision of the new Heaven to dim.

Disturb us, Lord, to dare more boldly to venture on wider seas where storms will show your mastery; where losing sight of land we shall find the stars. We ask you to push back the horizons of our hopes; and push into the future in strength, courage, hope and love.

(Attributed to Sir Francis Drake)

Knowing God

> The true vision and true knowledge of what we seek consists precisely in not seeing, in an awareness that our God transcends all knowledge and is everywhere cut off from us by the darkness of incomprehensibility.
>
> (Gregory of Nyssa, 330–95)

Edward is always telling me how God loves space. 'He must do, for he made so much of it.' He continues in this vein: 'God loves space. Physicists have discovered that the solidity of matter is an illusion created by our senses. Actually, 99.99 per cent of every object is "empty" space. This is the space between the atoms compared with their size, and there is as much space within each atom. Each object is a little universe; you are like a galaxy of stars. Between most objects in space there are great distances. God loves space.' Edward is more fascinating on this subject than I am able to convey. He reminds me that although we can never capture the God of space in the smallness of our minds, we can 'make' space for him in our hearts and lives. Reflect on this lovely prayer from the Hebrides:

> Wilt Thou not yield me vision,
> Lord of Grace,
> Of that vast realm
> Of unhorizoned space

> Which is Thy heart
> That heart-room makes for all?
> (Alistair MacLean, *Hebridean*
> *Altars*, Edinburgh, 1937, p. 101)

We are forever tempted to try to enclose God in the cage of our understanding, but any god so enclosed would be a graven image. It is simply not possible to comprehend fully a God who is beyond our comprehension. As the prophet Isaiah has God say:

> My thoughts are not your thoughts,
> nor are my ways your ways, says the LORD.
> For as the heavens are higher than the earth,
> so are my ways higher than your ways
> and my thoughts than your thoughts.
>
> (Isaiah 55.8–9)

Moses, in his desire to know God, asked God, 'Who shall I say that you are?' so that he could convey this to the people of Israel. He wanted to know God's nature, to be able to describe who he is. But God's otherness cannot be captured in thoughts or words. His reply to Moses, 'I AM WHO I AM', is full of mystery and invites Moses, and us, to seek to get to know him better (Exodus 3.13–22). The more we learn about God, the more carefully we will want to handle words about him, knowing that we cannot define him or tie him into a theological formula. All our doctrines are only pointers to the mystery of God: if they were demolished, God would still exist!

The more we discover of God, the more we realize there is to discover; the deeper our relationship with God, the greater our understanding of the riches that may be ours. In all our dealings with God there are always new depths to plumb and heights to ascend; there is always a sense of 'beyond'.

During my time at grammar school, in a desire for a deeper understanding of life – I hardly dare describe it as an awareness of God – I started going to St Michael's Church in Alnwick. Soon afterwards I joined a friend in attending the church choir, and the rehearsal during the week before the Fourth Sunday in Advent particularly sticks in my memory. It began at 6.30 p.m. I walked through a cold dark churchyard full of headstones in fear and trembling. A lively imagination can often be a bother! Inside the dim church, the choir stalls were in a pool of light about as far away from the door as possible, and I had a feeling of moving towards illumination and safety. We would spend most of the rehearsal on carols but first there was the anthem to be sung on Sunday. Its words were taken from the epistle for the day, 'Rejoice in the Lord always; and again I say, rejoice' (see Philippians 4.4). The choirmaster made us practise the anthem over and over until he felt we had mastered it. He came across to me while the singing was in progress, put his face close to mine and said, 'Rejoice, boy! Let me see you smile when you sing this. Show that you are glad that God is here!' I was terrified and found it hard to smile, look at the music and sing, but the words of that anthem became the first section of Scripture I truly learned. These words, committed to memory, entered my heart. Singing over and over, 'Rejoice in the Lord', 'the Lord is at hand' and 'be anxious of nothing' in worship helped me to know their reality deep in my being, and not only to acknowledge and rejoice in a presence but to smile because of it. Perhaps this is what Psalm 43.6 (*Common Worship: Daily Prayer*, Church House Publishing, 2005) means when it says, 'O put your trust in God; for I will yet give him thanks, who is the help of my countenance, and my God.' Can trust in God affect not only the way you look at the world but also the way you look? Sometimes a good simple exercise is to follow the advice of my choirmaster: 'Smile, for God is here.'

After the rehearsal, I could not sleep for thinking about the words of the anthem and hearing again and again in my mind, 'Rejoice, for the Lord is at hand'. The choirmaster had also explained how 'Emmanuel' told us that God is with us, and later in life I would realize that Advent is about being more alert and awake to the One who comes. It is an invitation to know that God is with us at every moment and that he actively seeks us out. I also mused on what the choirmaster had said about smiling because God is with me. In the darkness of my room I at last went to sleep, but not before I felt the joy of being in the presence of God.

Years later, I would be greatly interested in 'recital theology' – songs, hymns and rhythmical prayers that help to deepen our awareness and give us words to help us express what is, in fact, almost inexpressible. Prayers and hymns that have a rhythm or a beat are easily remembered and not only help us to say something about our feelings and awareness but also deepen that awareness. Letting the words vibrate not only on our lips but also in our hearts and lives increases their impact. Later, only a snatch of the tune can bring back the memory of the words, the feelings and the occasion.

Another musical event that really moved me was the first time I heard Handel's *Messiah* in St Michael's Church. The music seemed to enfold me, expressing itself in sounds rather than words. I found it very restful and peaceful, and when the Hallelujah Chorus began, I had a strange awareness of being in the presence of the God who is eternal, 'who shall reign for ever and ever'. It was something I can scarcely put into words – more than an emotion or a new piece of knowledge but rather as if the eyes of my heart had been opened, and I was aware with my whole being that I was in God's presence and enfolded in his love. Time and again in our lives we are given the opportunity to know that 'we dwell in him and he in us'. If we leave space, if we are alert and keep the eyes of our hearts open, the God who we imagine to be far off will make himself known, about us and within us. But though the anthem 'Rejoice in the Lord' and the Hallelujah Chorus bring back fond memories and remind me that God is with me, I cannot automatically conjure up an awareness of his presence simply through thinking of these pieces of music. But then, consider the advice given to the children at the end of *The Lion, the Witch and the Wardrobe*:

> I don't think it would be any good trying to get back through the wardrobe door to get the coats. You won't get to Narnia again by *that* route . . . Yes, of course you'll get back to Narnia again some day . . . But don't go trying to use the same route twice. Indeed, don't *try* to get there at all. It'll happen when you are not looking for it. And don't talk too much about it even among yourselves. And don't mention it to anyone unless you

find that they've had adventures of the same sort . . . Keep
your eyes open.

(C. S. Lewis, *The Lion, the Witch and the Wardrobe*,
HarperCollins, 2001, p. 203)

This is great advice, about not trying too hard – in fact, about
not trying, full stop. Sometimes our very prayers are so busy
that they prevent us being aware that God is seeking to speak
to us. We do not get to know him because we are too busy
talking. We do not realize his presence because we are too
actively searching for him. The advice of the Professor is,
'don't talk too much . . . Keep your eyes open.' Similar advice
comes in the Psalms: 'Be still, and know that I am God!'
(Psalm 46.10). In the stilling of our activity, we make space
in our lives for God to enter and be known.

We hear in the story of Moses how, though God has
appeared to Moses in the burning bush, spoken to him on
the mountain and revealed his power in the wilderness, Moses
longs for more. He wants to be granted a vision of God's
glory in all its fullness. In our own prayer times, it is only
right to long for more of God's presence and glory, to seek
to be still and more deeply aware of him. God's response to
Moses is that no one can look into the face of God and live.
However, he tells Moses that his glory will pass by, though
Moses will no more be able to look at it fully than he could
look into the sun. God will shield him from the fullness that
would more than blow his mind, and once God has passed,
Moses will be able to gaze at his back (see Exodus 33.18–23).
We are often only aware of God's presence and glory in
hindsight: we may go through an experience and only later
realize how good God has been to us, how he was with us

even when we did not see him or communicate with him. The glory of God is often depicted in art as rays streaming forth from a sun covered by cloud. The sun is still there, though hidden from our sight, and we still receive its benefits. *The Cloud of Unknowing* author is aware of how the cloud mystery hides the fullness of God, who is nonetheless ever present: 'To our intellect God is evermore incomprehensible . . . By our love he may be gotten and holden: by thought never' (ed. Evelyn Underhill, London, 1922, p. 89).

At this stage it would be easy to give up. Why bother trying to get to know God if he is incomprehensible? Yet in a sense, getting to know God is like getting to know anyone: you have to be willing to spend time with them and to give them something of yourself. 'By our love he may be gotten and holden'. There is a great difference between knowing about God and actually being able to say you know him, as is true of any relationship. We can know about people by reading about them and hearing others talk about them. We may even see them in action, but we can hardly know them without being with them and giving them our undivided attention. We need to allow them to communicate to us, and that will come about through a silent offering of ourselves, our attention and our love. Only then can our relationship become personal. To get to know God we will learn about him through the Scriptures, through the lives of holy people, through those who bear witness to his love. If we are fortunate, we will be taught to pray not only in fixed words but from the depth of our hearts. Often hymns and psalms can help us to express our desire and love for God, and it is good to learn prayers that help to tune our whole being to the reality that he is with us. The Celtic peoples of the Hebrides often used such prayers at the beginning of the day and while they were at work. This morning one is called 'God's Aid':

> God to enfold me,
> God to surround me,
> God in my speaking,
> God in my thinking.
>
> God in my sleeping,
> God in my waking,
> God in my watching,
> God in my hoping.
>
> God in my life,
> God in my lips,
> God in my soul,
> God in my heart.
>
> God in my sufficing,
> God in my slumber,
> God in mine ever-living soul,
> God in mine eternity.
>   (*Carmina Gadelica*, Vol. 3, ed.
> Alexander Carmichael, Scottish
>   Academic Press, 1976, p. 53)

I like the way each line begins with the word 'God': God is the subject, not an object, and the prayer is an affirmation of his presence rather than a request for anything. Using a prayer like this over a period of time gives it a new depth and meaning. A friend of mine recently said to me, about my use of the Psalms and Celtic prayers, 'You remind me of hitting a nail with a hammer. You cannot drive it home at once, but by regular repeated actions and love you arrive where you want to be.' This is well illustrated in a story about Alexander Carmichael as he was collecting the prayers for *Carmina Gadelica*. One evening an old man, while carried away with the love of God, uttered a singularly beautiful 'going to sleep' prayer and allowed Dr Carmichael to take it down; early the next morning, the old man travelled a round distance of 26 miles to exact a pledge that 'his little prayer' should never be allowed to appear in print. 'Think ye that I slept a wink last night for what I had given away? Proud, indeed, shall I be if it gave pleasure to yourself, but I should not like cold eyes to read it in a book.' Dr Carmichael handed the transcription back, to be burned there and then. The prayer was a song of the heart, and if pressed on to paper, some of its life would be lost.

In a like manner, Carmichael relates that when the people of the Isles came out in the morning to their tillage, their fishing, their farming, or any of their other various occupations, they would say a short prayer, called 'The Path of Right'. These people were at home with God and knew that God was at home with them. Each day they would turn to him to give their love and know his love for them. This was a wonderful mystery that they felt a stranger might not understand.

If the people feel secure from being overseen or overheard they croon, or sing, or intone their morning prayer in a pleasing musical manner. If, however, any person, and especially if a stranger, is seen in the way, the people hum the prayer in an inaudible undertone peculiar to themselves, like the soft murmur of the ever-murmuring sea, or like the far-distant eerie sighing of the wind among trees, or like the muffled cadence of far-away waters, rising and falling upon the fitful autumn wind.

(*Carmina Gadelica*, Vol. 3, pp. 48–9)

'The Path of Right' is another expression of being in the presence of God:

> My walk this day with God,
> My walk this day with Christ,
> My walk this day with Spirit,
> The Threefold all-kindly:
> Hò! hò! hò! the Threefold all-kindly.
>
> My shielding this day from ill,
> My shielding this night from harm,
> Hò! Hò! both my soul and my body,
> Be by Father, by Son, by Holy Spirit:
> By Father, by Son, by Holy Spirit.
>
> Be the Father shielding me,
> Be the Son shielding me,
> Be the Spirit shielding me,
> As Three and as One:
> Hò! hò! hò! as Three and as One.
>
> (*Carmina Gadelica*, Vol. 3, p. 49)

There is a need for us all to come before the presence of God in such a way throughout the day. How can we begin to know him if we do not speak to him? Our prayers should not be restricted to a single period or one place but should be strengthened by turning to God often during our daily activities. It is not surprising that we do not feel God's presence in church if we have ignored it throughout the week. Short little darts of love, directed at God, are a wonderful way of our keeping in contact with the One who is with us. Getting to know the presence of God is always a cause for rejoicing, and an occasion for alleluia.

As the illustration of the old man's 'going to sleep' prayer showed, there was a very deep feeling among the Celts that nothing important could be captured on paper. Caesar said of the Druids that they considered it improper to commit into writing something that was living. This is very much in line with the Tao expression, 'He who speaks does not know, he who knows does not speak.' The Orthodox Church also has a saying: 'As soon as we start speaking of the mysteries of God, we hear the gates of heaven closing.' Yet we seek to communicate that which is beyond words and to share with each other the presence and power of God that is beyond description. This should remind us that it is necessary to be still and quiet in God's presence – to make space in our lives, free from noise and activity, for God to speak. In any relationship, it is a sign that we are at home when we can be silent and enjoy each other's company.

We also need to realize that just as others communicate with us by what they do, God communicates with us in and through what he has made. The world teems with mystery and wonder, waiting to lead us into the mystery of God. But if we are unaware of the otherness of creation around us, which we can see, we will hardly be sensitive to the unseen God.

God, who made man that he might seek him – God whom we try to apprehend by the groping of our lives – that self-same God is as pervasive and perceptible as the atmosphere in which we are bathed. He encompasses us on all sides, like the world itself. What prevents you, then, from enfolding him in your arms? Only one thing: your inability to see him.

(Pierre Teilhard de Chardin, *Le Milieu divin*, Collins Fontana, 1975, p. 46)

Yuri Gagarin was the first man to enter space, on 12 April 1961. When he returned to earth he said, 'I looked and looked but I did not see any god there.' One of the Orthodox priests in Moscow responded, 'If you have not seen him on earth you will never see him in heaven.' This is the world God has given to us; it is in this world that he is with us and it is through this world that he challenges us and speaks to us.

In getting to know God we need to discover for ourselves that the world came into being through him; that he made us and we are his. It is good to give thanks each day for our own being and for all of the wonders of Creation, then to rejoice that God made the world out of his love and for his love. We are precious in his sight and he keeps us in his care every moment, even when the days are dark:

Though the dawn break cheerless on this isle today,
My spirit walks upon a path of light.
For I know my greatness.
Thou hast built me a throne within Thy heart.
I dwell safely within the circle of Thy care.
I cannot for a moment fall out of Thine everlasting
   arms.
I am on my way to glory.

(Alistair MacLean, *Hebridean Altars*, p. 55)

Our relationship with God will not deepen if we deny the
world, thinking we would do better to substitute the spiritual
for the material. We may sometimes have to detach ourselves
from certain things for a while in order to know God better,
but this would be the case whenever we want to give something our attention. I am a great believer in fixing times and
places to meet up with friends, for without the planning we
can fail to get together. In the same way I believe that we need
to have fixed times and places to acknowledge the presence
of God and give him our undivided attention. But we must
always be aware that we can meet God at any time and in
any place, for he is always with us.

> Man has every right to be anxious about his fate so long
> as he feels himself to be lost and lonely in the midst
> of created things. But let him once discover that his
> fate is bound up with nature itself, and immediately,
> joyously, he will begin his forward march.
>
> (Pierre Teilhard de Chardin,
> *Hymn of the Universe*, Fontana, 1974, p. 98)

Know that God waits for your return. He has not forgotten
you: he holds you in his heart. Accept the invitation to come
into his presence, to place yourself personally today before
God. You can use a hymn or words of Scripture to remind
you that God is with you, though in time you will be content
to delight in him in silence. That great spiritual guide, the
Curé d'Ars, tells a lovely story of a certain peasant being
asked why he was so long in prayer. The reply was, 'I look
at him and he looks at me.' In similar vein, I like the comment Mother Teresa of Calcutta made when she was asked,
'What do you do when you pray?' 'I listen to God,' she replied.

The enquirer then enquired, 'What does God do?' and the answer came, 'He listens to me.' In the stilling of our lives we give God the opportunity to speak to us. In giving him our attention we can get to know him and enjoy his presence.

In a wonderful homely way this awareness of God's presence was expressed by a woman from Kerry in the south-west of Ireland. 'Where is heaven?' she was asked. 'It lies about a foot-and-a-half above the height of a man,' she replied, suggesting that to enter God's kingdom you do have to stretch yourself a bit, but it is there for those who reach out to it, wherever they are.

Too often we have relegated God and the kingdom of heaven to the far distance, when God and the kingdom are close at hand. There is no need to go in search of God for, in the words of St Paul, 'In him we live and move and have our being' (Acts 17.28). It is important to speak to him, listen to him and speak about him. When we discover the presence of God, we will see all things in their depth and in their beauty. But if we ignore the presence that vibrates in every atom, then we will live a lie and become lonely and alone. If our deep sense of loss is shared by everyone around us, then there is a danger we will accept our blindness for normality. The call to thrust out a little is the call to become more sensitive, more alive to what is around us. It will ask us for a while to turn our backs on our normal routine, but the reward for doing this is to discover a depth to life that has been passing us by. Everything that is, is full of mystery, is holy. Nothing is profane, all is sacred, for all belongs to God and is able to reveal glory. We must learn again to stop and to give our wholehearted attention to this wonderful world in which we live and its Creator.

Exercises

Fix a time and a place to be still before God. Keep to this time and place for at least a week, if not longer. Then in the stillness seek to give yourself, your attention, your love, to your Creator. Rest in his presence; make yourself at home with him. God does not require gifts or even words: he simply wants you. Seek to give yourself to him and know that he gives himself to you. Take to heart the words, 'Be still, and know that I am God!' (Psalm 46.10).

If you find your mind wanders too much, use a sentence to centre yourself on God, such as: 'God, you love me: I seek to love you,' or 'God, you give yourself to me: I seek to give myself to you.'

In time you should be able to centre yourself simply by saying 'God', and re-placing yourself in his presence.

Think upon these words:

> . . . the closeness of our union with him is in fact determined by the exact fulfilment of the least of our tasks. We ought to accustom ourselves to this basic truth until we are steeped in it, until it becomes as familiar to us as the perception of shape or the reading of words. God, in all that is most living and incarnate in him, is not far away from us, altogether apart from the world we see, touch, hear, smell and taste about us. Rather he awaits us at every instant in our action, in the work of the moment. There is a sense in which he is at the tip of my pen, my spade, my brush, my needle – of the heart of my thought.
> (Pierre Teilhard de Chardin, *Le Milieu divin*, Collins Fontana, 1975, p. 64)

Pray

O gracious and holy Father,
give us wisdom to perceive you,
intelligence to understand you,
diligence to seek you,
patience to wait for you,
eyes to behold you,
a heart to meditate upon you,
and a life to proclaim you,
through the power of the Spirit
of our Lord Jesus Christ.

     (St Benedict, *c*.480–*c*.550)

Loving

———•◆•———

'Would you know our Lord's meaning in this? Learn it well. Love was his meaning. Who showed it to you? Love. Why did he show it to you? For love. Hold fast to this, and you shall learn and know more about love, but you will never need to know or understand about anything else for ever and ever.' Thus did I learn that love was our Lord's meaning.

(Julian of Norwich, *Enfolded in Love*,
Darton, Longman and Todd, 1980, p. 59)

For Christmas 2011, Denise and I received a jar of pickle that reminded me of one of the great learning moments in my life. It began in my grandma's tiny kitchen when she had just prepared the dough for a batch of bread. There was a good smell of baking in the house and it was a joy to inhale the aroma. I asked, 'Granny, why is your bread better than anyone else's?' I could see her almost shine at the question. 'It is because I have a secret ingredient and not everyone puts it in their baking.' 'What is it?' I asked. 'It is love, dear, it is love. I bake love into my bread. If you put love in, it always makes a difference.'

At the time I could hardly say I understood this, but I have often since discovered the difference love makes. I am aware of how far removed wrapped, sliced bread usually is from the home-baked variety. I am also aware that baking and cooking always reveal something of the personality of the cook. I actually heard one cook say, 'I was feeling bitter today and I put some of my troubles into the things that I have cooked. They do not taste the same as usual.' All we deal with in the course of a day is influenced by our love or our neglect of it. The Christmas jar of pickle was given to us in a little cloth bag decorated with flowers and a little girl holding out a heart. I knew it had a secret ingredient, for it was made as a gift of love. Hidden behind the list of spices and fruit, love was waiting to be received and known. Each gift offered in love, no matter how simple, is a sacrament.

In J. D. Salinger's *Franny and Zooey*, Franny, a 20-year-old student, has returned home from theological college a nervous wreck. She is not eating and keeps compulsively reciting prayers. Her mother, Bessie, is concerned for her and in loving care prepares and brings a cup of chicken soup. Franny pushes it away. This makes her brother Zooey angry and he says:

'I tell you one thing, Franny. One thing I know. And don't get upset. It isn't anything bad. But if it is the religious life you want, you ought to know right now that you are missing out on every single religious action that is going on in this house. You don't even have sense enough to drink when somebody brings you a cup of consecrated chicken soup – which is the only kind of chicken soup Bessie ever brings to anybody around this madhouse. So just tell me, just tell me, buddy. Even if you went out and searched the whole world for a master – some guru, some holy man, to tell you how to say your Jesus prayer properly, what good would it do you? How in hell are you going to recognize a legitimate

holy man when you see one if you don't even know a
cup of consecrated chicken soup when it's right in front
of your nose?'

(J. D. Salinger, *Franny and Zooey*,
Penguin, 2010, pp. 127–8)

One of the great ways of learning to love is by first recog-
nizing the love we are given. In an ideal world we are created
out of love and for love. Our parents may not often express
their love in words, but they demonstrate it by offering their
time and attention, by giving us themselves. Many a mother
pours love into her cooking and her care for the family. If
she were not able to do this, the work would soon become
a chore. Before we ever learn to love we are loved, and it is
this free gift – neither earned nor deserved – that gives strength
and meaning to our whole being. It comes from God; through
our parents; from relatives and friends. It makes life worthwhile, and in return for this gift, nothing is asked except that
we respond to love and give love in return. Where love is
poured in, let it flow out to others and infuse all you do with
purpose and meaning. When life is a struggle and everything
appears to be against you, remember that you are loved.
When prayer seems to die and words will not come, seek
to respond to love. John Chrysostom said, 'Find the door to
your heart, it is the door to the kingdom of God.' In love we
discover God, in love the doors of our whole being are
opened to a new life, a new world, and we move towards
healing and wholeness.

I have always been fascinated by the healing power of love,
illustrated here in a story from the Outer Hebrides. Life was
hard for a woman and her son, living in a small croft by the

sea. The boy was ill and whatever his mother did for him, whatever treatments he was given, he did not get better. The illness turned the two of them in on themselves, in the way health problems often do. The mother was anxious that her son was fading away, and they began to feel the meaning of the words 'in the midst of life we are in death'. They struggled to survive. Then one morning they found an injured swan on the shoreline which looked as if it was starving to death. With some difficulty they carried it to their croft and cared for it. They reached out to this injured creature and gave it their attention and their love. And as the swan regained its strength, so the boy began to recover. His healing kept pace with that of the bird. The swan had drawn the little family out of themselves and out of illness, and by the time the bird flew, the lad was well on the way to fullness of health. In looking after another being, in giving their love to it, the mother and the boy found healing in their lives.

This is not an unusual story, for love is often a great source of healing. When visiting in hospital, I would often meet people whose wounds would not heal, whose illness found no cure. Though pain was eased, recovery was often halted. I became aware that many such patients had no visitors and often felt uncared for and unwanted. Though there were people around them who looked after them and were concerned about their needs, healing often only really began when they discovered that they were missed by friends and neighbours. One lady in such a plight, who had a wound that would not heal, received a surprise visit from her daughter. For some reason they had lost contact with each other, and the daughter only discovered from someone else that her mother was in hospital. She arrived in tears and said how sorry she was not to have come sooner, promising to visit every day and to have her mother stay with her as soon as she was well enough to leave hospital. From the time of her daughter's first visit, the mother's recovery was rapid. She realized she was loved and wanted: she felt life was worthwhile and began to mend. There are many similar stories. Most of our folk tales tell of love healing, of love transforming beasts, of love setting prisoners free, of love conquering the power of evil. Such tales are expressions of the redeeming and healing power of love. They also reveal how life is impoverished without love.

As I said earlier, the ideal is that we all receive love from the moment we are born. We learn love at our mother's breast and from the way we are cared for and often sacrificed for: through the way our parents give themselves for us and for our well-being. We are born for love and to share love. Love gives us confidence in life; it makes us able to venture out, to look beyond ourselves. Love changes the way we view each other and the world around us. But because we are human and not perfect, sometimes the ideal is lost.

Not everyone receives love or is born into a loving home. Many, sadly, carry scars of being unloved, or of being injured in love or betrayed by loved ones, and their confidence and trust, as a result, are diminished. Children denied love often hold themselves in low esteem, and do not thrive in the same way as those who are surrounded by love. They will be hampered by these feelings until they are loved and accepted by someone for who they are. In reaching out in love we can actually give new life to those who are struggling just to survive.

For many years Denise and I were short-term foster parents. We looked after children while a mother was in hospital or needed respite care. Most of these youngsters were loved by their parents and concerned about being away from them, but occasionally we had a child who felt unloved by anyone. Usually they were either desperate to please or, alternatively, they railed against everything. Some expressed self-loathing, making it difficult to help them or to build up their self-esteem in the short time they were with us. We learned, time and time again, that love has great power to heal and to bestow confidence. One child, radiant after struggling for a while, was able to say, 'It's great here. You really do like me.'

Denise has always had a weakness for wanting to help the rejected and the weak, and this comes through in her response to animals too: I was always having to persuade her not to buy runty lambs at local sheep sales! We did keep sheep, and a friend who was a shepherd gave us lambs to look after. We found it interesting that the ewes used a special, more tender voice than usual to communicate with their young. And we quickly learned that lambs taken away from their mothers and bottle fed did not thrive so well: though we offered food and attention, we could not fully replace the relationship with the mother. Similarly, people who stayed with us who had been deprived of love in some way often did not thrive even as adults. I can think of two people in particular who longed for relationships with their mothers, though both had rejected their children long ago. One used to search for his mother every now and again, feeling his life was incomplete because he did not know her and had not experienced her love. The other, a woman in her twenties, did trace her mother but sadly discovered that the woman did not want anything to do with her. For a good while after this, the young woman was disturbed. We all know that if love – or even the hope of love – is removed from our lives we are quickly diminished, and that if we do not experience love it is hard to find love to pour out. I understand what St Paul means when he said, 'Without love I am nothing.' Indeed, we are in a desperate situation, for without love we cannot enter into fullness of life.

The Secret Garden by Frances Hodgson Burnett is a favourite children's story of mine about love and the lack of it. There are three main characters. Mary Lennox, now orphaned, has never really experienced the love of her parents, though materially she lacks nothing. The lack of love in her life is revealed in her attitude to people and in her looks. Colin Craven, her cousin, has also lost his mother, and while his father provides for him, he hardly ever sees his son and could not be described as loving. As a result, Colin has lost the will to live: he scarcely leaves his bed and believes he cannot walk. The third character, Dickon, is the brother of the maid Martha, and from a large but poor family. There is nonetheless a lot of love in this family, reflected in the way that Dickon, who is a St Francis type of character, talks to the birds and loves life and the world around him. Through their relationships with each other, and the Secret Garden that they all love, the children learn to love and to live fully. With this loving comes healing and new strength for Colin, and a much better appearance and attitude from Mary. Here is a telling passage from early on in the book, when Mary is asked by Martha, her maid:

'What would Dickon think of thee?'

'He wouldn't like me,' said Mary in her stiff, cold little way. 'No one does.'

Martha looked reflective again.

'How does tha' like thyself?' she inquired, really quite as if she were curious to know.

Mary hesitated a moment and thought it over.

'Not at all – really,' she answered. 'But I had never thought of that before.'

Martha grinned a little as if at some homely recollection. 'Mother said that to me once,' she said, 'she was at the wash-tub an' I was in a bad temper an' talking ill of folk, an' she turns around to me an' says "Tha' young vixon, tha'! There tha' stands saying tha' doesn't like this one antha' doesn't like that one. How does tha' like thysel'?" It made me laugh an' brought me to my senses in a minute.'

(Frances Hodgson Burnett, *The Secret Garden*,
MDS books/Medisat, 2003, p. 63)

There is no doubt that love changes everything. Denise in her love for me confirms my worth, challenges my actions, but above all celebrates my being. When I am confirmed in love, I am encouraged. I feel secure as a person and have confidence in what I am doing, which gives me the energy I need to achieve things. There is a great strength in love that helps us through challenging times. Many people crumble in difficulties, not because they are not strong enough to survive, but because they feel alone. We can all feel safer in the dark if a loved one is with us. Of course, there are also times when Denise confronts me and questions my actions.

This is not to criticize, unless in a positive way, but to guide me and assist me in what I am aiming to do. Love does not like to see us go off in wrong directions or do what is not worthy of us. Love speaks out, not to force us to change but to help us see more clearly. In this sense love improves our vision of ourselves and of the world. A strong love is always able to give constructive criticism, and in love we should be able to accept this. But above all, Denise celebrates that I am me. She rejoices in my existence, my worth and my uniqueness. (How amazing that she loves *me*!) Denise does not want me to be a copy of someone else: she wants me to have the courage to be who I am and she is willing to share her life with me. Together, our life is a celebration of love, though being human, we sometimes fall below this ideal.

All forms of love are precarious. Love can easily become selfish: when we use another person for mere pleasure, or seek to dominate them, we are loving no one but ourselves. When we see the other as an object of desire for the gratification of our senses, or as a way of gaining power, we are self-absorbed. Love in its fullness can never be egocentric. It is not the urge to possess, to have or to own; it is not self-regarding or self-referring, but rather self-giving, always reaching out to others. Such love is risky and makes us vulnerable. This is illustrated well by the love of God in Jesus, who was betrayed and then crucified by those to whom he came to give himself.

There is an important distinction between selfish love, which lusts for power and control over others, and a healthy self-love. If we do not respect and pay attention to our own being, it is unlikely that we will be respectful or attentive towards others: if we have a low opinion of ourselves, this will be reflected in how we react to others. Time and again I have seen selfish people transformed by the discovery that they are loved and lovable: when they know this, they can pour themselves out in love to others. For love does not have its centre *in* but *outside* the self. Love is an outpouring of our being, an attending to the other, a valuing of the worth of the other. Sadly, 'I love you' in our language often means, 'I want to have you, possess you, and own you.' A far deeper and more passionate love is shown in the giving of oneself to the other. Such love is respectful, gentle, and bestows value on the beloved. Spaniards, who are known to be a passionate people, have more than one term for what we loosely call 'love'. *Te quiero* suggests desire, need, lusting after, even seeking to control. *Te amo* does not have the same undertones, but is rather an expression of outgoing love, of the willingness to give and to serve. True love opens up for us a whole new way of living and looking at the world. Such love is only possible when we reach out to another with our whole being; it is the sort of outpouring love through which God created the world. We were created for love and out of love, and the very source of our being is love. In our most fragile moments, we may be aware that we are made of dust and to dust we shall return, but in the depth of our being we *know* that we are more. We have not been created out of nothing but out of love, and our journey will end in 'lovers meeting'.

Early in life we learn to love not only our parents but the world around us. We give our attention to things that attract us and spend time discovering new wonders. The world of a child is often full of self-giving love, but as we grow and become busy, we tend to lose the capacity to respond so generously. Often we have been encouraged by dualistic thinking to turn our backs on the world in pursuit of 'spirituality', though those with a proper scientific training, working with matter and the physical side of things, usually have respect for the mysteries of life and an appreciation of creation. As do artists, gardeners and poets! But people who imagine themselves religious sometimes treat the world with a high disregard as if it did not matter. There is a lovely example of this from eighth-century Ireland. Samthann is the abbess of Clonberry, and a student called Dairchellach, who is obviously seeking to opt out of his work, comes to her and says, 'I propose to give up study and give myself to prayer.' It sounds pious and noble, but Samthann shrewdly replies, 'What then can steady your mind and prevent it from wandering if you neglect spiritual study?' Failing to secure permission, the student then says, 'I wish to go abroad on pilgrimage.' To which Samthann replies, 'If God cannot be found on this side of the sea, by all means let us journey overseas. But since God is near to all those who call upon him, we have no need to cross the sea. The kingdom of heaven can be reached from every land.' Our love for God is shown and expressed in the way we treat his Creation.

The world is the means by which God communicates with us. Through the world and our life experiences we become open to wonder and awe, learn of the mysteries of this life, and discover his love. One of the greatest mistakes of converts or new believers is to think that they can turn their backs on the world. It is God's Creation, and if our attitude towards the least of his creatures is wrong, then our attitude to God will be too. Some of the worst crimes ever have been committed in the last two centuries in the name of progress.

Our environment, seas, rivers, rainforests and atmosphere have all suffered, as humans have sought to dominate, possess and control rather than learn to give of themselves. Many so-called 'primitive' societies cannot understand our belief that we can own and sell the land. There is a thought-provoking saying from the Cree Indians of America: 'When all the trees have been cut down, when all the animals have been hunted, when all the waters are polluted, when all the air is unsafe to breathe, only then will you discover you cannot eat money.' Similarly, Indian Chief Seattle, after whom the city of Seattle is named, said, during the assembly in 1854 when the Indian tribes were preparing to sign away, under duress, the land they lived on: 'Whatever befalls the earth befalls the children of the earth. The air is precious for all of us share the same breath. We know that this earth does not belong to us; we belong to the earth.'

The Celtic Christians of our land would have understood this well. Columbanus in the sixth century said: 'He who tramples on the earth, tramples on himself.' Love for creation in general – for animals, plants, minerals, the earth and the stars – is not greatly developed in Christian teaching and theology. Too often we write this world off, or give the impression that we believe we are meant to put everything under our control. Yet this is the world God has given to us: this is where we live and where God reveals his love. We may not feel that we have much encouragement to love the world with heart and soul, but in giving ourselves to the beauty of the sunrise and the starry skies, to the rolling sea and the fields of barley swaying in the wind, we open ourselves to a glimpse of glory that is of God. A good exercise in God's love comes from Ignatius Loyola's 'Contemplation for Achieving Love':

Love consists in a reciprocal inter-change, the lover hand-
ing over and sharing with the beloved his possessions . . .
Recall the good things I have had from creation . . . See
God in his creatures –

in matter, giving them existence,

in plants, giving them life,

in animals, giving them consciousness,

in men, giving them intelligence.

More, he makes me his temple . . .

Think of God energizing, as though he were actually
at work, in every created reality, in the sky, in matter, in
plants, and fruits, and herds and the like . . .

Realize that all gifts and benefits come from above.

(Quoted in T. Corbishley, *The Spirituality of
Teilhard de Chardin*, Fontana, 1971, p. 30)

Today we do not give enough time to the glories that are
around us. We are caught up in an outlook that is full of
agendas and tasks. We might be in a lovely place but decide
to ring someone on our mobile, or feel desperate to catch
the latest episode of a reality TV show. We fill our lives with
activities and rarely sit in silence – even at home there is
always the temptation to turn on the radio or have a CD
playing in the background. But love is shown through being
attentive, through the giving of ourselves:

The substance of love of our neighbour is attentiveness.
It is an attentive way of looking . . . the soul empties
itself of itself in order to receive in itself the being that
it is looking at, just as he is, in all his truth.

(Simone Weil, 'Reflections on the Right Use of School
Studies', in *Waiting for God*, Fount, 1977, p. 53)

Concerning such neighbours, I like the words of someone who has had a bad press within the Church, the declared heretic Pelagius:

> When Jesus commands us to love our neighbours, he does not mean only human neighbours; he means all the animals and birds, insects and plants, amongst whom we live. Just as we should not be cruel to other human beings, so we should not be cruel to any other species of creature. Just as we should love and cherish other human beings, so we should love and cherish all God's Creation.
>
> (Robert van de Weyer, *The Letters of Pelagius*, Little Gidding Books, 1995, p. 71)

The Celtic Christians were in no doubt that they were to love God's world and so encounter the revealed love of God. Their view of creation encouraged them to seek to live in harmony with what was around them rather than dominate it. And so should we, who believe in God the Creator, show that we love the world that our Father has given to us. We should delight in matter and in our humanity. And we should listen to God speaking to us as he gives himself to us in love, and seeks our love for him and for his world.

We all need to make friends; we are not meant to live alone. And as we develop loving relationships, their effect should extend outwards in ever-increasing circles. The warmth of friendship is essential to all of life. As Augustine said: 'Without a human being who is our friend, nothing in the world appears friendly to us.' Friendship, the gift of loving and being loved, is powerfully transforming and should be celebrated. It is always an occasion for alleluias.

Exercises

Be still and affirm that you are in the presence of God: rest in his love. Relax, let go of any tension. Check that each part of your body is at rest. Remember that you cannot make God come to you, for he is already with you and he loves you: enjoy his presence.

Look around you and affirm that this is God's world; he has made it, and it belongs to him.

Know that he gives his love to you through the world and not apart from it. God uses the world to speak to you. Give thanks for the world and then look at an area where you feel God is prompting you to become involved. You may like to look at an ecological event, the loss of wildlife, or an area of a natural disaster. What is God saying to you through it? What might he require of you? If possible, promise that you will do your best to help in the situation.

Rest again in God and give thanks for his love for all his Creation.

Take your time to think over these words and seek to put them into practice:

'Love a man even in his sin, for that is the semblance of Divine Love and is the highest love on earth. Love all God's creation, the whole and every grain of sand in it. Love every leaf, every ray of God's light. Love the animals, love the plants, love everything. If you love everything, you will perceive the divine mystery in things.'

117

By loving, man gains new respect for everything in God's world. Thus 'we must love not occasionally, for a moment, but for ever.'

(Fyodor Dostoevsky, The Brothers Karamazov,
Book 6, Chapter 3)

Pray

Pray in love for the good world God has given to us. You may like to use these words thoughtfully and slowly. Seek to visualize each thing that you offer and do not forget to offer God the most precious gift you can: yourself in love.

GLORIFICAMUS TE

I offer Thee
Every flower that ever grew,
Every bird that ever flew,
Every wind that ever blew,
   Good God!

Every thunder rolling,
Every church bell tolling,
Every leaf and sod!
   Laudamus Te!

I offer Thee
Every wave that ever moved,
Every heart that ever loved,
Thee, my Father's Well-Beloved.
   Dear Lord.

Every river dashing,
Every lightning flashing,

Like an angel's sword.
　　Benedicimus Te!

I offer Thee
Every cloud that ever swept
O'er the skies and broke and wept
In rain, and with the flowerlets slept.
　　My King.

Each communicant praying,
Every angel staying
Before Thy throne to sing.
　　Adoramus Te!

I offer Thee
Every flake of virgin snow,
Every spring of earth below,
Every human joy and woe.
　　My Love!

O Lord! And all the glorious
Self o'er death victorious,
Throned in heaven above.
　　Glorificamus Te!
　　　　　　(Ancient Irish Prayer)

God is our lover

Beloved, let us love one another; because love is from God; everyone who loves is born of God and knows God. Whoever does not love does not know God, for God is love. God's love was revealed among us in this way: God sent his only Son into the world so that we might live through him. In this is love, not that we loved God but that he loved us and sent his Son to be the atoning sacrifice for our sins. Beloved, since God loved us so much, we also ought to love one another. No one has ever seen God; if we love one another, God lives in us, and his love is perfected in us.   (1 John 4.7–12)

While working on Holy Island, I was privileged to meet many wonderful people. Life was busy but I was given help by local retired clergy to care for tourists and pilgrims, while two very dedicated men took turns to look after the churchyard and the fabric of the church. These people offered their time and talents out of love. So did a group of nuns from the community of Our Lady of Namur, which is committed to 'taking our stand with poor people, especially women and children in the most abandoned places'. They came one summer, saw how busy I was, and promised to return each year for a fortnight to help. Over the years I met some wonderful sisters, and it was with sadness that I heard in February 2005 of the murder of 73-year-old Sister Dorothy. She had been on her way to a meeting with poor farmers in the Amazon when two gunmen came to the remote forest settlement and shot her six times. In the early 1980s, Sister Dorothy became involved in sustainable agriculture and forestry schemes in the Amazon, teaching peasant farmers to conserve the resources of the land rather than exhaust them. She also helped them to secure legal titles to land that others were eager to take from them. Needless to say, Sister Dorothy's work brought her into conflict with the commercial interests of those determined to exploit the forest's valuable tropical hardwoods: it was estimated that nearly 90 per cent of the timber was being illegally logged. All opponents of this deforestation faced intimidation, and Sister Dorothy had been receiving death threats since a group of landowners had tried unsuccessfully to bring a prosecution against her the year before. But she believed that her work was to show God's love and care for these oppressed and neglected people, and for the Amazon itself. This brave witness cost Sister Dorothy her life. The giving of ourselves in love is often costly, as we know from the sacrifice of Christ, but it is what we are created to do. We reveal our closeness to God when we give ourselves in love.

And the possibility of giving ourselves in love comes from knowing that we are loved: indeed, 'beloved'. One modern translation of the above passage begins, 'My dear friends' and thus misses the whole point, for to be 'beloved' is to be loved by God. God loves us before we love him. That is the great message of the gospel: we are already loved. Before we ever learn to love, we are loved. Without earning or deserving it, we are given the free gift of love, and all we are asked in return is to give and respond to love. In love we discover God, and the doors of our whole being are opened to a new life, a new world. There is a lovely description of this in Susan Hill's novel, *Air and Angels*. A middle-aged don, who is about to be elected as Master of his college, falls in love with Kitty, a much younger woman. They go to the seaside for the day, and on the beach he sees the world around him with new eyes in a way he has never experienced before:

All of his past, the old interests and concern, dropped quite away from him, and his old self was sloughed off, like the skin. And looking about him he saw the world re-created, all things were strange but new, brave and infinitely rare and beautiful to his eyes. He looked at the sea and sky, at the stone beneath his feet, and the shimmer on the far horizon, and the bird balanced on the post ahead, and he knew he had never seen their like before, all were miraculously new to him.

(Susan Hill, *Air and Angels*, Mandarin, 1991, p. 263)

In love we move out of our own petty self as we give ourselves to the other. Let love flow out, and as you do, more love will flow in. This sounds wonderfully romantic, but we must be aware that in this fallen world it can prove costly. Jesus came to reveal God's love to the world. He showed care for the outcasts and lepers rejected by society, but he was made an outcast himself. The God of love was squeezed out of his world and nailed to a cross. Love can be crucified. But nothing – not even death – can separate us from the love of God in Christ Jesus.

Though there was not much coverage in England, someone who inspired me when I was still in Sunday school was canonized by Pope Benedict XVI on 11 October 2009. Father Damien of Molokai, 'the leper priest', was born in Belgium in 1840. He joined the Sacred Heart Fathers at the age of 20, and four years later was sent to Honolulu in Hawaii where he was ordained priest. During his nine years there, he became aware of more and more people suddenly being sent off to the leper colony on the island of Molokai – in great distress and with no hope of returning. So in 1873, out of his love for God and these poor people, Damien volunteered to go to Molokai to minister to the lepers. He set about improving the appalling conditions, seeking more medical assistance for the island, and overseeing the building of orphanages (he had a great concern for the children), hospitals, clinics and churches. In expressing his love in this way, he gave his life to the outcasts and the poor, for he became a leper himself in 1885 and died four years later. Gandhi declared that Damien was an inspiration for his social campaign in India, saying that 'if you don't find God in the very next person you meet, it is a waste of time looking for him any further'. In love, we are to see Christ in others, and to be Christ to others.

This story from the life of St Martin of Tours has always moved me deeply. On a severely cold night in a winter that was proving fatal to many, especially the poor, the soldier Martin met a beggar at the city gate of Amiens. Martin had no money, only the military clothes he stood up in and his weapons, while the poor man was almost naked. All who passed by ignored his calls for help, for there were too many beggars for people to take notice of one in particular. But Martin stopped and looked in love upon the man. What should he do? He had already given his money away and had nothing left of use except the cloak he was wearing. Quickly deciding to share this, he drew his sword, divided the cloak into two equal parts and gave half to the beggar. As Martin walked away with only half a cloak around him, many mocked his foolishness. Yet others felt a twinge of conscience because they had more than Martin and had done nothing. That same night, when Martin lay down to sleep, he had a dream in which he saw Christ wearing half a cloak. He was told that this was the cloak with which he had clothed the poor man, and then he heard Christ say in a loud voice to the angels of heaven, 'Look what Martin who is still a catechumen has clothed me with this day.' Love is costly but it is through love that we reflect the divine in us and see it in others.

There are moments in all our lives when something happens to open our eyes or deepen our normal sense of perception: moments that, if we allow them, will change our lives for ever. Such experiences are hard to put into words because if a person has not had a similar experience they will not really know what we are talking about. Martin was sure that he had met Christ in a beggar, and he would not be the first or the last to encounter the living Lord. Saul met Christ on the road to Damascus: he saw nothing but a blinding light yet he heard the voice that said, 'I am Jesus, whom you are persecuting' (Acts 9.5). A nurse I know who works in a hospice says that she gets her strength to care from seeking to serve Christ in the other. The truth is that the incarnation, though unique in Christ, is not a past event but an eternal reality! The Incarnate Lord is present in this world; he wants to meet with us and we may encounter him on our travels in the most unexpected of disguises. I have a friend who works in the prison service and is often asked, 'Why do you bother with such people?' His reply is always much the same, 'I believe in the God of love and he does not want even the least of his loved ones to be lost or neglected.' Occasionally, if my friend feels that the person he is speaking with might understand, he quotes Jesus, saying, 'I was in prison and you visited me: as much as you did it to the least of these you did it to me.'

Francis of Assisi is often rather romantically portrayed surrounded by the birds he talked to and the wolf he tamed. We have no trouble seeing him minister to animals or ordinary, needy folk, as we can all love the lovely. But accepting the ugly and the 'unlovable' often takes a great act of will and a great heart. When Francis was suddenly confronted by a leper needing his love – someone scorned and rejected by society and with no apparent beauty – the look and smell of the leper repulsed him and made him feel sick. Francis knew he could not ignore this man; he had to master his feelings and look beyond the obvious to the extraordinary depth below. He gathered the leper into his arms and enfolded him in brotherly love. And as he held the leper, Francis knew he was embracing Christ and that Christ was embracing him. The great Other had come to Francis in the poor man before him, and that poor man's face was the face of Christ: 'Beloved, let us love one another; because love is from God; everyone who loves is born of God and knows God.'

Each of the people I have mentioned in this chapter discovered in depth the sacrament of the incarnation: the 'Word made flesh and dwelling among us'. Their eyes were opened to the reality of the words of Jesus: 'Just as you did it to one of the least of these . . . you did it to me' (Matthew 25.40). Each had the ability to see Christ in the other and at the same time to be Christ to the other. One day I made a hospital visit to someone who had lost most of his friends through his unloving attitude towards others; later that day a tramp called at the vicarage. We gave him a meal and a place to stay for the night in what was once a stableboy's dwelling. After breakfast the next morning he went on his way, and it was just after this that I wrote:

> You are the caller,
> you are the poor,
> you are the stranger
> at my door.
>
> You are the wanderer,
> the unfed,
> you are the homeless
> with no bed.
>
> You are the man
> driven insane,
> you are the child
> crying in pain.
>
> You are the other
> who comes to me.
> If I open to another
> you are born in me.
> > (David Adam, *The Edge of*
> > *Glory*, Triangle, 1985, p. 34)

When we meet Christ in the other, it is life-changing – a privilege that demands we treat every individual with respect, for we cannot pick and choose where we might encounter Christ next. Though our meeting might begin with one individual, our experience will soon affect our dealings with everyone.

Alistair MacLean tells of a noblewoman of the Hebrides who had given food and shelter to a visitor. Before he left he asked her:

> 'Tell me the secret of your exceeding gentleness.' At this the lady mused for long, her eyes downcast; then answered softly as one waking from a lovely dream, 'There is no secret – only – I am always at His feet and He is always in my heart.'
>
> (Alistair MacLean, *Hebridean Altars*, Edinburgh, 1937, p. 77)

But while love encourages us to be sensitive towards one another, to care for and desire to help each other, to turn away from God and in on ourselves spells disaster. St Augustine expresses this well:

> God whose kingdom is the whole universe that
>   our senses cannot perceive;
> God whose kingdom lays down the laws for the
>   kingdoms of this world;
> God from whom to stray is to fall
> and to whom to return is to rise up,
> in whom to remain is to rest on a firm
>   foundation.
> To leave is to die,
> to return to you is to come back to life,
> to dwell in you is to live . . .
> To go away from you is to be lost,
> to seek you is to love,

to see you is to make you our own.
Faith urges us towards you,
hope guides us
and love unites us to you.
        (*Praying with Saint Augustine*, SPCK, 1987, p. 88)

The story of the Prodigal Son (Luke 15.11–32) is one of the greatest stories in the world. It has such wide appeal because it is a story everyone can relate to. We are all in danger of taking love and our homes for granted. We often demand as of right what should be given freely. The son says to his father, 'Give me what belongs to me.' He cannot wait. Then he sets off to a distant country. When self-will rules, we choose to step out of the kingdom of God, break with the Father and live in a world that has no reference to God or his grace. Many can say with St Augustine:

How different are my days
from the days of the Lord!
They are 'my' days
because I took them for myself,
intoxicated as I was by my reckless independence
which led me to abandon him . . .
        (*Praying with Saint Augustine*, p. 26)

In the distant country, the Prodigal is far from the influence of his father's love. He spends all his money on loose living and in time, as always happens, his resources run out. Having wanted to go it alone, he is now alone. The love he tries to buy is not true love, and he is forced to do what any Jew would abhor: look after some pigs. In a state of starvation, he finds himself eating pig food and this proves to be a turning point. Realizing that even his father's servants are better off than he is, he decides, 'I will arise and go to my father.' Perhaps it was with these words in mind that St Augustine wrote: 'God from whom to stray is to fall and to whom to return is to rise up.'

Every time we discover that God loves us, we take part in a resurrection. We rise above mere matter and our own self-centredness and know ourselves loved and valued as the unique being we are. Such experiences ought to be repeated on a daily basis. Then, when we are raised from the final death, we will realize that our new life is not altogether unfamiliar. The truth is that we have the chance to enjoy life in all its fullness *now*. As Harry Williams writes in *True Resurrection*:

> When we begin to recognise the power of the resurrection present in the ordinary gritty routine of our daily lives, then we shall see for ourselves that all that separates and injures and destroys is being overcome by what unites and heals and creates. We shall no longer have to ask where and when this happens, for we shall have first-hand experience of it as we live as ordinary folk in the ordinary world.
>
> (H. A. Williams, *True Resurrection*, Mitchell Beazley, 1979, p. 13)

The Prodigal is willing to admit his sinfulness; he is willing to be a slave in his father's house, for that would be far better than his current predicament. He sets off, but long before he reaches home his father runs out to meet him, propelled by a love that pays no heed to this supposed indignity to his status as a gentleman. The father had been waiting and longing for the return of his son, and embraces and enfolds him in a love that has never wavered. Everyone is invited to celebrate, 'for this son of mine was dead and is alive again: he was lost and is found!' There is no judgement, only rejoicing in love.

So does our Father act, 'drawing near to us as we draw near to him' (James 4.8). We may have left him but we are always in his heart. The joy of his own homecoming is described by Augustine in one of the best-known passages from his *Confessions*:

> I was slow to love you, Lord,
> your age-old beauty is still as new to me:
> I was slow to love you!
> You were within me,
> yet I stayed outside
> seeking you there;
> in my ugliness I grabbed at
> the beautiful things of your creation.
> Already you were with me,
> but I was still far from you.
> The things of this world kept me away: I did not
>   know then
> that if they had not existed through you
> they would not have existed at all.
> Then you called me
> and your cry overcame my deafness;
> you shone out
> and your light overcame my blindness;
> you surrounded me with your fragrance
> and I breathed it in,

so that now I yearn for more of you;
I tasted you,
and now I am hungry and thirsty for you;
you touched me,
and now I burn with longing for your peace.

> (*Confessions* X.27,
> *Praying with Saint Augustine*, p. 19)

Place yourself in the love of God: turn to him knowing that he loves you. Let the love of God enfold you, then see that love rippling out as it enfolds his Creation, your loved ones and everyone you meet. A good way to begin each day is to turn to God and his love, and you may like to learn this little prayer of St Augustine:

> O love ever burning and never extinguished,
> charity set my heart on fire with love for you.
> (*Confessions* X.19)

Realize God's love, rest in God's love, rejoice in God's love and make this an occasion for alleluias.

Exercises

Relax, rest in the presence and love of God. Make sure you are comfortable and without any tension anywhere. Affirm the reality of God with your lips, then in your thinking and then in your heart.

God is with you.
God cares for you.
God loves you.

Say to yourself, 'I am loved by God more than I can either conceive or understand.' Let this fill your soul . . . and

never leave you. You will soon see that this is the way
to find God.

(Henri de Tourville, *Letters of Direction*, in Michael
Mayne, *This Sunrise of Wonder*, Fount, 1995, p. 241)

Think upon these words of Hilary of Poitiers from his
'Treatise on the Trinity':

I came to see that there is no space without God: space
does not exist apart from God. God is in heaven, in hell
and beyond the seas. God lives in everything and enfolds
everything. God embraces all that is, and is embraced
by the universe: confined to no part within it he encompasses all that exists.

(Quoted in Robert Atwell, *Celebrating the Saints*,
SCM Press, 2004, p. 37)

Pray

God, I seek to share this moment with you,
my life with you.
God, I give myself in the stillness,
I have nothing else to offer.
God, I seek to give you my attention,
my heart, my mind, my whole being.
God, I desire to see you in and through your world
and in my life.
God, I long to know you, your presence,
and to have a relationship with you.
God, I give you all that I am in love,
as you give yourself to me in love.
God, I rejoice in you and your love
today and for ever.

Enjoying life

He who binds to himself a joy
Doth the wingèd life destroy;
But he who kisses the joy as it flies
Lives in Eternity's sunrise.
(William Blake, MS Notebook,
'Several Questions Answered')

I watched Alec, a young man in his early twenties, after he came home from a long day at work drained of energy. He did not notice the beauty of the evening or how nice the meal was that he was served. He had a lawn to mow but did not feel up to it. He appeared lethargic. He switched on the television and switched off from everyone in the room. He slumped in his chair. Then he received a call on his mobile. A young woman in whom he delighted asked if he would like to have a game of tennis. At that moment it was as if he had been reborn. An amazing change came over him as new powers rushed into his body, and even his appearance altered. Alive and ready for action, he bounded up the stairs and was ready in double-quick time. Soon he was out and playing tennis. I knew the young woman was a very good player and the game would be strenuous.

They played tennis for the allotted hour and when he returned, Alec told me he had lost the game but had a wonderful time. He was full of joy and energy. Even now, though it was late, he decided it would be good to cut the lawn before he settled down for the night. I watched him in the fading light. He looked radiant. Coming in later he said simply, 'I enjoyed that.' I think his words applied to cutting the lawn as well as playing tennis and being with a beautiful young woman.

Now, I could have offered to play tennis with him, but I do not think that would have relieved his weariness. The young woman had a quality I could not offer at that moment. She drew him out of himself, and in drawing him out she inspired joy as well as love. We cannot create joy, but we can live the sort of life that keeps us open to the possibility of it occurring. Emily Dickinson expresses this well in her love for the world:

> But were it told me – Today –
> That I might have the sky
> For mine – I tell you that my Heart
> Would split, for size of me –
>
> The Meadows – mine –
> The Mountains – mine –
> All Forests – Stintless Stars –
> As much of Noon as I could take
> Between my finite eyes.
>
> The Motion of the Dipping Birds –
> The Morning's Amber Road –
> For Mine – to look at when I liked –
> The News would strike me dead.
>
> (Emily Dickinson, 'Before I got
> my eye put out', *Complete Poems*,
> Faber and Faber, 1970, p. 155)

This poem is not about possessing in the sense of owning things, but about loving, sharing and enjoying. The joyous person is the one who lives a life of love because she knows she is loved. Without this love, joy is fleeting at best. In a sense it is a by-product of the way we live and the view we have of life. If we seek to possess, conquer or dominate, joy and love will elude us. It is in the giving of our attention and the opening of our lives to the other that love can be poured in, and we can experience joy. Joy is not something we can create, which is why it is recognized as a gift of the Holy Spirit. Joy is richer and deeper than happiness, though not necessarily separate from it. Sometimes there is a great sadness about 'party people' who are forever chasing after happiness. The etymological root of the word is, after all, 'hap', meaning 'chance, fortune'. Robert Burns, who often chased after happiness himself, wrote:

> But pleasures are like poppies spread,
> You seize the flower, its bloom is shed;
> Or like the snow falls in the river,
> A moment white – then melts for ever;
> Or like the Borealis race,
> That flit ere you can point their place;
> Or like the rainbow's lovely form
> Evanishing amid the storm.
> (Robert Burns, 'Tam O'Shanter',
> 1791, lines 59–66)

Yet we can have sudden moments of joy at any time. I can remember one dull day in late spring when we had two children staying with us in the vicarage. They were lounging about, not sure what to do, when I went out to the hen house to collect eggs. A hen who had been sitting for a while decided to go for a wander, and out of curiosity I picked up one of her warm eggs and put it to my ear. Immediately I heard the chick inside the egg cheep. What a joy to share! I ran back into the vicarage and said to the children, 'Come quickly, follow me.' It was the beginning of an adventure for them. Fortunately the hen was still off her eggs, so I picked one up and said to the first child, 'Put it to your ear and listen.' I'm sure she thought this a bit strange but cautiously she did as she was asked. There was a moment of silence, then with a great smile, she handed the egg to her friend. The chick inside the egg obliged again, and the second child laughed openly. 'It's wonderful: it's a miracle.' The egg was carefully put back and they watched the hen return to her sitting, before dancing around the garden to celebrate what they had experienced. Their joy was spontaneous but they wanted to share it. They wanted to get back to school and tell everyone. One of the children said, 'No one will believe it!' A few days later, they danced round the garden again when they saw the chicks with the mother hen. Their joy may not have lasted long but I felt they would remember it for ever.

The Bible makes a distinction between joy and pleasure. Time and again the Scriptures warn that the chasing of pleasure alone will not lead to joy or fulfilment. In Ecclesiastes 2.1–11 we are shown how pleasure-seeking left the writer feeling empty and disillusioned. There is an awful description in Proverbs 14.13: 'Even in laughter the heart is sad'. The Greek word for pleasure is the word from which we get 'hedonism', which is used to describe self-centred pleasure-seeking. St

Paul foresaw distressing times coming when people will be 'lovers of themselves, lovers of money' and 'lovers of pleasure rather than lovers of God'. He believed such an attitude would lead to boastfulness, arrogance, abusive behaviour and brutishness (2 Timothy 3.1–5).

Joy, unlike happiness, does not depend on chance, though it is related to our awareness of what is around us and to feeling loved and of worth. I have seen and known people in extreme poverty express joy because they have someone who cares for them. I have watched the faces of people who are in pain, or even terminally ill, light up when their hand is clasped by someone who loves them: there is radiance and joy in the interchange. A hymn I have always found a moving expression of such joy is 'O Love that will not let me go' by George Matheson. It was written in about five minutes on the eve of his sister's wedding when Matheson was aged 40. Many years earlier his own fiancée had broken off their engagement when she discovered he was losing his sight. Though blind at 20, Matheson was able to continue his studies thanks to a very good memory and the assistance of his sister. By 1868 he had his own parish at Innellan, on the western shore of the Firth of Clyde, and it was from here that he wrote in 1882:

> O Love that will not let me go,
> I rest my weary soul in thee;
> I give thee back the life I owe,
> That in thine ocean depths its flow
> May richer, fuller be.
>
> O light that followest all my way,
> I yield my flickering torch to thee;

My heart restores its borrowed ray,
That in thy sunshine's blaze its day
May brighter, fairer be.

O Joy that seekest me through pain,
I cannot close my heart to thee;
I trace the rainbow through the rain,
And feel the promise is not vain,
That morn shall tearless be.

Each of these verses has deep meaning. Matheson knew a love that never left him, the love of his sister and of his God. He could always rest in and give himself to that love. His sister had been eyes for him, as God was his light in the darkness. Matheson was not freed from the sorrows of life, but he knew a joy that sought him even through pain. There is always a potential for joy in our lives, whatever our circumstances.

Two young teenagers once accompanied me into the small paddock at the vicarage, which contained an old potting shed. We used it as a hen house and also to shelter our two sheep. I had asked them if they would like to see a lamb being born, knowing that the ewe was due. The potting shed had its own cosiness, and during the short wait, I could see that they were totally caught up in this new experience. They watched wide-eyed and almost in silence as the lamb arrived, was tidied up by its mother and then struggled to its feet. They saw it suckle for the first time. Then, quite overawed by the whole event, the older lad said, 'It's a blooming miracle!' It was so good to share in their wonder and awe, and I was reminded of Walt Whitman's poem:

Why, who makes much of a miracle?
As to me, I know of nothing else but miracles,
Whether I walk the streets of Manhattan,
Or dart my sight over roofs of houses toward the sky,
Or wade with naked feet along the beach, just in
   the edge of the water,
Or stand under trees in the woods,
Or talk by day with any one I love, or sleep
   in the bed at night with any one I love . . .
Or watch honey-bees busy around the hive of a
   summer forenoon . . .
Or the wonderfulness of the sundown, or of stars
   shining so quiet and bright,
Or the exquisite, delicate, thin curve of the new
   moon in spring . . .
To me every hour of the light and dark is a miracle,
Every cubic inch of space is a miracle,
Every square yard of the surface of the earth . . .
What stranger miracles are there?
               (Walt Whitman, 1819–92, 'Miracles')

It is a sad day when we stop being aware of the miracles of life, when we cease to wonder, or find we no longer respond with awe and joy to the mystery of being. I often meet with people who are serious, full of their problems and seem to have lost the ability to smile. There is little joy in their lives because they are out of harmony with what is around them. They may be more concerned with what they possess, or fail to possess, than the joy of being alive. Empty or desperate, unfulfilled and lacking in purpose through chasing after the wrong things, they are like T. S. Eliot's 'hollow men', and belong to 'the mass [of people who] lead lives of quiet desperation' (described by Henry Thoreau in his 1854 book, *Walden*).

It would seem that we are often defeated by the gravity of the world when we might be responding in delight. I am not suggesting that we should run away from problems, but I do feel we need to learn not to be serious all the time! This change in attitude will come through looking outwards and becoming aware of what is really all around us – in discovering once more that there is an otherness in all of life that cannot be defined:

> A rediscovery of the supernatural will be, above all, a regaining of openness in our perception of reality. It will not only be, as theologians influenced by existentialism have greatly overemphasised, an overcoming of tragedy. Perhaps more importantly it will be an overcoming of triviality. In openness to the signals of the transcendence the true proportions of our experience are rediscovered. This is the comic relief of redemption; it makes it possible for us to laugh and play with a new fullness.
>
> (Peter Berger, *A Rumour of Angels*, Penguin, 1970, p. 119)

One dark January morning, I met a local poacher and mole-catcher at the paper shop. He had seen the northern lights during the night and was describing with great joy how they danced across the skies. He went on to enthuse about how wonderfully the earth was adapted for life. But a programme about the northern lights on television, which had also been wonderful to watch, had left him cold. The presenter's explanation of the 'lights' had 'treated them as if they were a problem'.

Much contemporary literature and cinema reflects on life as a problem and presents a grey, grim society of joyless people. Only occasionally does there seem to be a happy ending or a rescue from the darkness. And the truth is that many of us find bleakness interesting because our lives feel bleak. Dietrich Bonhoeffer, who was arrested by the Nazis and later executed, after two years in prison, on 9 April 1945, was aware of how joyless much of life had become for many people, and saw this reflected in the drama and literature that was being produced. He wrote these words from prison:

> On the whole, all the newest productions seem to me to be lacking in *hilaritas* – 'cheerfulness' – which is to be found in any really great and free intellectual achievement. One has always the impression of a somewhat tortured and strained manufacture instead of creative activity in the open air.
>
> (*Letters and Papers from Prison*, SCM Press, 1971, p. 189)

Later on, returning to this theme, he wrote encouragingly: 'Now that's enough for today. When shall we be able to talk together again? Keep well, enjoy the beautiful country, spread *hilaritas* around you, and keep it in yourself too!' (p. 232).

We need to be aware of what is around us, to enjoy what we can and to encourage others to share in that joy. It is good to rejoice in the gift of each new day, in the fact that we are alive, and in the mystery of life. We must never allow life to become dull. The first time I heard John Osborne's play, *Look Back in Anger*, I wanted to shout 'Yes! Yes!' as I heard these words:

> How I long for just a little ordinary, human enthusiasm. Just enthusiasm, that's all. I want to hear a warm, thrilling voice cry out 'Hallelujah! Hallelujah! I'm alive!' . . . Oh, brother, it's such a long time since I was with anyone who got enthusiastic about anything.
>
> (John Osborne, *Look Back in Anger*,
> Faber and Faber, 1957)

There is always something thrilling about being with enthusiastic people who show commitment, love and joy in what they do. They seem truly alive and full of energy, with a light in their eyes and a warm way of relating to others. They can often make what one thought of as a dull subject seem exciting and full of riches, and are a joy to be with. It is no accident that the word enthusiasm comes from *en theou*, the Greek for 'being in God'. The joy that comes with enthusiasm cannot be kept to ourselves, for it is meant to flow out to others. The seventeenth-century religious poet, Thomas Traherne, tells us: 'You never enjoy the world aright, till you so love the beauty of enjoying it, that you are covetous and earnest to persuade others to enjoy it' (Meditation 31, *Centuries of Meditations*, ed. Bertram Dobell, London, 1948, p. 31).

Each day I try to take nothing for granted but seek to rejoice in the newness of each day and the freshness of each encounter. When possible I attempt to share what I have seen and experienced with those around me. For when we enjoy life and find fulfilment in what we are doing, we have a huge effect on others. Joy-filled people are radiant people, and when the days are dark we need to be among them.

Augustine saw that true joy comes in sharing the joy of God, and asked:

> O greatest joy,
> joy that is above all joys,
> when shall I share in you
> and see my Lord who dwells in you?

For Augustine, to rejoice in God was truly an occasion for alleluias.

Exercises

Be still in the presence and love of God. Rest in him, let go of all anxiety. Allow your body and mind to rest. Do a check over each part of your body to be sure that you are as comfortable and rested as possible. God does not ask for gifts, he asks for your attention, for you to be open to him. When the mind wanders from God, bring it back to him by affirming his presence and his love. You may like to say. 'You, Lord, are in this place and your presence is love.' Rejoice in his presence.

After a while you may like to turn your attention to something of God's Creation and, in his presence, give him thanks for it and its uniqueness. Rejoice that it is his and he has made it.

Say, 'You, Lord, are in all that you have made and your presence is joy.'

Here are some words by Thomas Traherne to think about:

> Your enjoyment of the world is never right, till every morning you awake in Heaven; see yourself in your Father's Palace; and look upon the skies, the earth, and air as Celestial Joys.
>
> (Meditation 28, *Centuries of Meditations*, p. 19)

Pray

Lord, renew our spirits and draw our hearts to you,
that our work may not be a burden to us, but a delight.
Oh, let us not serve you with a spirit of bondage as slaves,
but with the cheerfulness and gladness of children,
delighting ourselves in you, and rejoicing in your work.

(Benjamin Jenks, 1646–1724, adapted)

The joy of God

O be joyful in the Lord, all the earth;
serve the Lord with gladness
and come before his presence with a song.

Know that the Lord is God;
it is he that has made us and we are his;
we are his people and the sheep of his pasture.

Enter his gates with thanksgiving
and his courts with praise;
give thanks to him and bless his name.

For the Lord is gracious; his steadfast love is
  everlasting,
and his faithfulness endures from generation
  to generation.
(Psalm 100, *Common Worship: Daily Prayer*,
Church House Publishing, 2005)

While I lived on the North Yorkshire moors I would often listen to the local 8 a.m. weather forecast. One day the forecast began, 'It is bright and sunny across the county and will stay that way all day.' In fact, where I was it was dull, grey and almost dark: there was no sign of the sun at all! The forecaster's world and mine did not seem to be quite the same, but I trusted him and decided to take the car out of the valley and up the nearby hill outside Castleton. I had my lights on, as the visibility was so poor. But as I climbed, there was a gradual suggestion of brightness and eventually the car burst into brilliant sunshine. I found myself in another, radiant world. A little further on, I could look down and see that the fog had become beautiful white clouds, filling the valley as snow had done in the last ice age. It was a wonderful sight. I could have stayed at home in the gloom, but my decision to seek a new perspective had made a huge difference to the day. Over the years, when life seems grey, I have learned to 'enter his gates with thanksgiving and his courts with praise'.

The life of the Hebridean crofters of the past was often very tough, and they received little reward for their mostly repetitive labour. There were times when they were not sure how long they could survive, especially in hard winters when it could be very dangerous fishing in stormy weather. Yet they were people of song, and learned to rejoice in what was around them and in the love, care and presence of God:

> Even though the day be laden and my task is dreary, and my strength is small, a song keeps singing in my heart. For I know that I am Thine. I am part of Thee. Thou art kin to me and all times are in Thy hand.
>
> (Alistair MacLean, *Hebridean Altars*, Edinburgh, 1937, p. 60)

God created the world out of his love and for his love. Having been given life on earth, surely it is only right that we allow the light of his presence to shine upon us and rejoice in the wonders of creation. The Jews recognize this, and the Talmud tells us, 'In the world to come each of us will be called to account for all the good things God put on this earth which we refused to enjoy.' God has bestowed life upon us in order that we might enjoy his world and praise its Creator.

A group of children came to Holy Island from a town in the Borders. It was a day for exploration and adventure, and they were all given various small projects. Some went to look for 'Cuthbert's Beads' (a fossil found on the beaches); some spent time in the ruined priory; some visited the lime kilns and saw seals swimming near the harbour. Yet another group went to sketch the upturned boats that are used as sheds. Later, I told them stories of Aidan and Cuthbert. The children had brought a picnic lunch to eat outside, and by the end of the day they were looking quite sunburnt. Gathering in the church before their departure, the teacher, without any prompting, sought a response of praise for the day. 'What did you think of it?' she asked one lad. 'It was guid, Miss.' She pointed to others and two in turn replied, 'It was guid, Miss.' Wanting to elicit a more expansive response, she enquired, 'Has anyone any more to say than that?' A hand shot up. 'It was verra guid, Miss.' At this there was a burst of laughter and all the children clapped their hands. Their response reminded me of the Genesis story of the Creation.

At the very beginning of the Scriptures, we find after each act of creation the refrain, 'And God saw that it was good' (Genesis 1.4, 12, 18, 21, 24). It is as if the writer wants us to look at each part of creation with him and affirm its goodness. At the end of the sixth day, God surveys what he has made and finds it 'very good'. It is not a bad exercise for us to look at the Creation each morning and echo God's delight in what he has made. I use these lines from *Common Worship* daily:

> As we rejoice in the gift of this new day,
> so may the light of your presence, O God,
> set our hearts on fire with love for you,
> now and for ever.
> (*Common Worship: Daily Prayer*, p. 115)

I then have a few moments of rejoicing in the newness and freshness of the morning. Sometimes I call to mind the words of Job, who describes creation as 'when the morning stars sang together and all the heavenly beings shouted for joy' (Job 38.7). The book of Proverbs continues this theme and tells of the divine wisdom at the creation of the earth: 'I was daily his delight, rejoicing before him always, rejoicing in his inhabited world and delighting in the human race' (Proverbs 8.30–31). God invites us to share in this joy and in his presence. The Westminster Catechism asks, 'What is the chief end of man?' We are to reply, 'To glorify God and to enjoy him for ever.' We do this through delighting in his world, not in turning our backs on it or misusing it. The world is not to be despised but loved with the love God shows towards it. Our relationship with God should not centre so much around sin and the fall, but around delighting in what God has given to us, and his love.

There are some pretty dour and grave Christians who appear to say, 'If it is joyful, it is sinful.' But their reason for encouraging us to turn our backs on the world may be that they are afraid of feeling fully alive. I like to remember the words of a short prayer attributed to St Teresa of Avila: 'From silly devotions and from sour-faced saints, good Lord, deliver us.'

The Desert Fathers fled from a society full of pleasure-seekers who nonetheless appeared to be out of touch with the joy of life. In the desert, the Fathers revelled in God's Creation and in living simply. They worked hard and often suffered deprivations, but sought to enjoy the presence of God and his love. One declared, 'Joy is the echo of God's life in us.' Now that is something to think about! I am told that when you turn a television to where there is no programme transmitting, the 'snow' it often picks up is to some extent the reverberations of the Big Bang at the beginning of creation. In the same way, this Desert Father suggests that in expressing joy, we are echoing God's response to his Creation. This is a wonderful idea to explore, and in the dark days, when the clouds come down, there is much comfort in knowing that nothing 'will be able to separate us from the love of God in Christ Jesus' (see Romans 8.35–39). As Julian of Norwich wrote:

> It is God's will that we should rejoice with him in our salvation, and that we should be cheered and strengthened by it. He wants our soul to delight in its salvation, through his grace. For we are the apple of his eye. He delights in us for ever as we shall in him by his grace.
>
> (Julian of Norwich, *Enfolded in Love*,
> Darton, Longman and Todd, 1980, p. 13)

When I worked down the coal mine, I wore a lamp on my head. One of its effects was that when you turned to look at someone, their face lit up. I would later read how Moses' face shone when he came back to the people in the wilderness after being alone with God. In Psalm 34.5, the psalmist says of God, 'Look to him, and be radiant.' The same thought is expressed in Psalms 42.14 and 43.6: 'O put your trust in God; for I will yet give him thanks, who is the help of my countenance, and my God' (*Common Worship, Daily Prayer*). I used to say Psalm 43 every time I helped at Holy Communion. I often did this on a weekday, not long after coming home from working in the coal mine. It was then I particularly liked the words, 'O put your trust in God; for I will yet give him thanks, who is the help of my countenance, and my God,' for it reminded me of the shining of the pit lamp on a face. In the same way the radiance of God shines upon us. The psalmist was aware that looking at God would lift his spirit and transform his expression. A friend described knowing God as the best sort of facelift!

My links with the Anglican Church mean that I am used to singing and reciting the Psalms, and I know how many are about joy and rejoicing in God. I often use Psalm 16.11 as a thanksgiving: 'You show me the path of life. In your presence there is fullness of joy; in your right hand are pleasures for evermore.' I have become more and more convinced that to know God and his love is to be enabled to walk with confidence and to live life more adventurously.

There are psalms that have become part of my daily pattern of prayer. Psalm 95 (BCP), which begins, 'O come, let us sing unto the Lord: let us heartily rejoice in the strength of our salvation. Let us come before his presence with thanksgiving: and shew ourselves glad in him with psalms', delights in the fact that God made the world and us. It also reminds us of the danger of 'hardness of heart'. To share in God's joy it is necessary to keep our hearts open to him and to his world. To receive the gift of joy we have to be open to what God offers us.

Another psalm I often say in Morning Prayer is Psalm 100, which is a wonderful meditation on joy. I used to visit a church on the moors that was gloriously sited amid heather-clad hills, with a stream running past and a ruined castle nearby. It was a favourite place of mine, though in fact the church was damp and appeared neglected; it was a struggle to sing in and the preacher was not very inspiring! Yet inscribed on the east wall above the window was an invitation to 'come into his presence with thanksgiving'. I would think, why had I come to this little church? Not for the hymns or the surroundings. Not for the preacher, or the building. No, I had come to affirm that I was in God's presence; to kneel where generations had knelt and to offer myself as they did. I was here not for outward things but to rejoice in the Lord, and in so doing to discover afresh that all is in God. Rejoice in the fact that you are in God and God is in you. Rejoice that you are in the heart of God!

Psalm 100 was a courageous song for the Jews, for they often faced persecution. They knew what it was to spend time in the desert, in thirst and emptiness. It is often still necessary to pass through the deserts of this life before we come to the Promised Land, or to set aside our 'little pleasures' to make space for the glorious presence of God, and so be blessed through our worship with love, peace and joy.

The first line of the psalm suggests that the whole earth should rejoice in God. God's love is not restricted to Jews, churchgoers or the favoured few, but is for all people in all places. And God's mission, in which we are invited to share, is to reach out in love to everyone. Even the earth is invited to rejoice in God. There is that lovely passage in Isaiah where we read that 'the mountains and the hills before you shall burst into song, and all the trees of the field shall clap their hands' (Isaiah 55.12). This in its turn reminds me of the Hebridean woman who said:

> My mother would be asking us to sing our morning song to God down in the back-house, as Mary's lark was singing it up in the clouds, and as Christ's mavis [song thrush] was singing it yonder in the tree, giving glory to the God of the creatures for the repose of the night, for the light of the day, and the joy of life. She would tell us that every creature on the earth here below and in the ocean beneath and in the air above was giving glory to the great God of the creatures and the worlds, of the virtues and the blessings, and would *we* be dumb!
>
> (*Carmina Gadelica*, Vol. 3, ed. Alexander Carmichael, Scottish Academic Press, 1976, p. 25)

'Serve the Lord with gladness.' Within Judaism there are prayers for the doing of common tasks, and blessings are asked upon daily activities. In the same way, the Celtic Christians enjoyed working in God's presence and for God's glory. They were able to speak naturally to God in their daily tasks, and had prayers for arising, for lighting the fire, for milking, for setting off to work, for weaving, for ploughing, for fishing or for a journey. These people delighted in God and found it natural and easy to enter into his presence with a song or prayer.

I love to celebrate that I am alive: to celebrate the whole of creation, to celebrate the presence and love of God. In celebrating Holy Communion, I celebrate a communion with the earth, a communion with God, a communion with God through the earth, and a communion with the earth through God. In the bread and wine I give thanks and offer the world to God and I offer God to the world; I accept the world from God and God from the world. I celebrate that the whole of creation, from neutron to nebulae, is created by God and is God-filled. I can find God through his Creation and I can find a common union with Creation in God. God's way of giving joy to the world is through the giving of himself and through the 'ordinary' creation. The Communion, the common union, is a celebration of the at-one-ment: we are at one in our God with all of creation. Sadly I remember some words of Harvey Cox, who said that modern man was pressed 'so hard toward useful work and rational calculation he has all but forgotten the joy of ecstatic celebration' (Harvey Cox, *Feast of Fools*, Harvard University Press, 1969, p. 12). For this reason I wish more people would take to heart these words by G. K. Chesterton:

> You say grace before meals.
> All right.
> But I say grace before the play and the opera,
> And grace before the concert and the pantomime,
> And grace before I open a book,
> And grace before sketching and painting,
> Swimming, fencing, boxing, walking, playing,
>   dancing;
> And grace before I dip the pen in the ink.

'Come into his presence with a song' is an invitation, and represents one of the easier ways of rejoicing in God. You may have turned your back on God, like a prodigal son or daughter who has left home. You may have ignored God or felt that you have let your relationship with him slide. Know that God awaits your return in love. He has not forgotten you for he holds you in his heart. Accept the invitation to 'Come into his presence' and enjoy being with God, wherever you are. You do not need to go to church to come 'face to face' with him. Simply rest in his presence and give him your attention and your love. You may like to use a hymn or psalm to remind you that God is with you. At junior school, I can remember going to the Salvation Army for a while and singing this song:

> I am H.A.P.P.Y.
> I am H.A.P.P.Y.
> I know I am, I'm sure I am
> I am H.A.P.P.Y.

Then came verses on being L.O.V.E.D. and S.A.V.E.D. The chorus was always sung with joy and gusto and I delighted in it. No one ever tried to define these words for us; we were simply encouraged to experience what we were singing. We did not need to understand theories of the atonement to feel that being saved had something to do with being held in the love of God. It would only gradually dawn on me how my joy was bound up with being loved by God, who gave himself to me and for me. Songs like 'I am H.A.P.P.Y.' may seem simplistic, but they are grounded in the truth that God is our maker, our lover and our keeper, and that knowing this should give us great joy. I still find hymns, or 'recital theology', a wonderful way of expressing God's loving presence. The Celtic Christians knew its value and affirmed much of their faith and love through hymns and verse.

'Know that the Lord is God.' God alone is in control. I like the statement of the psalmist, 'Some put their trust in chariots and some in horses, but we will call only on the name of the Lord our God. They are brought down and fallen, but we are risen and stand upright' (Psalm 20.7–8, *Common Worship: Daily Prayer*). It reminds me that my father often put too much trust in horses and football coupons; sadly, many of his horses were brought down and fallen and his teams defeated! There are many things we might be tempted to put our trust in, whether health plans, security, money, popularity or ourselves. It is easy to delude ourselves that we are self-sufficient and independent. But the truth is that we need many things to survive that are not of our own making: water and air are two good examples. We also need each other, or we do not grow fully as people. And, of course, we need our living present God. For 'we are his: we are his people and the sheep of his pasture'. What a joy to affirm that we are God's Creation, and that all there is belongs to him. We do not know what lies ahead in life, but we can be sure who will be with us as we journey on.

> Wherever he may guide me,
> No want shall turn me back;
> My shepherd is beside me,
> And nothing can I lack.
> His wisdom ever waketh,
> His sight is never dim,
> He knows the way he taketh,
> And I will walk with him.
> (Anna Waring, 1823–1910,
> 'In heavenly love abiding')

'Enter his gates with thanksgiving'. One of the easiest ways to place yourself before God is through appreciating what has been given to you and acknowledging the love of the giver. It is almost impossible for a thankful heart to be a sad heart, and the ability to 'count our blessings' can move us out of emptiness and boredom and into joy.

'For the Lord is gracious; his steadfast love is everlasting, and his faithfulness endures from generation to generation.' Seek to make yourself aware of this reality. God is good and generous. He gives us life; he gives us love; he gives us himself. His love is an everlasting love, dependable and steadfast.

> I saw that God never began to love mankind. For just as man is destined to come to endless joy, and so crown God's delight in his work, so man in God's thought has always been known and loved. From him we come, in him we are enfolded, to him we return. We shall find in him our whole heaven in everlasting joy – and this by foreseeing purposes of the blessed Trinity since before time was. In this endless love man's soul is kept safe . . . In this endless love we are led and looked after and never lost. For he wills that we should know our soul to be alive, and that this life – through his goodness and grace – shall continue in heaven without end; loving him, thanking him and praising him.
>
> (Julian of Norwich, *Enfolded in Love*, p. 32)

Who needs more than this! Our journey through prayer, with the help of the wording from the prayer of St Augustine, has taken us along a rather straight path, and I am aware that life is not like this – although there is a natural progression from resting to seeing, from seeing to knowing, from knowing to loving and from loving to enjoying. Indeed, there may be times when we seem to be involved in all these activities at once, through our relationships with each other, with the world and with God. It is fitting to end with Augustine's words as he looked back on his life:

> There is one joy that is not granted to the wicked,
> But only to those who give you honour,
> For you yourself are joy.
> This indeed is happiness: rejoicing in you, about
>   you, for you, this and nothing else.
> Whoever believes that here is happiness other
>   than in you
> is pursuing something different,
> not the possession of true happiness.
>
> (*Confessions* X.22)

That knowing in its fullness is love and in this we rejoice. With this awareness we have many occasions for alleluias.

Exercises

Be still and quiet. Make sure that you are as comfortable as possible. Check over each part of your body and make sure it is free from being over-tense. Still the mind with a single phrase or affirmation of God's presence. You may like to use the following: 'You, Lord, are here: in you I rejoice.' Repeat this a few times with your lips, then in your mind. Finally, let it be repeated in love by your whole being.

Now slowly diminish the sentence while holding the whole of it in the words that are left.

> You, Lord, are here: in you I rejoice.
> You, Lord, are here.
> You, Lord, are.
> You, Lord.
> Lord.

Now rest in him and his love. If the mind wanders, bring it back with the single word, 'Lord'.

Think upon the words from the prayer of St Augustine, 'All shall be Amen and Alleluia' (page xvi), and know that this is for living now and for fulfilment in the fullness of life eternal. You may like to continue to use the words as a daily affirmation – and seek to live by them. Look at opportunities for resting, seeing, knowing, loving, enjoying, and the occasions for alleluia. Know that each occasion is an opportunity for meeting God.

We shall rest: Build times of rest into your day, and as part of that rest make space for God. Set aside a part of every day when you seek to rest in God, without the need of words. Know that you dwell in him and he in you.

We shall see: Teach yourself to look with the eyes of your heart: to give your undivided attention to the people you make contact with. Choose a subject each day, be it a person or a bird or flower, and give your full attention to what it is.

We shall know: Develop that knowledge that is more than book knowledge. Make sure you get to know God rather than just about him. Learn to commit yourself enough to have a personal relationship with your subject – and with those whom you love.

We shall love: Give thanks for all the people who have given their love to you: the people who have sacrificed for you and cared for you. Know that before you ever loved, you were loved, and are loved. Make sure, where you can, you return love with love. Learn and give yourself in love to what you do each day.

We shall praise: Come each day into his presence with thanksgiving. Rejoice in God's love and salvation. Rejoice that you are one with him: that he dwells in you and you in him. Rejoice in his Creation and in all the relationships you have with it. Each day give praise and thanks to God for something in your life or in the world, something new. Behold our end, which is no end, to celebrate life: to celebrate God and his love. Let all be 'Amen and Alleluia', until all of life is an occasion for alleluias.

Pray

O God, you are the light of the minds that know you,
the life of the souls that love you,
and the strength of the wills that serve you.
Help us so to know you that we may truly love you,
and so to love you that we may fully serve you,
whom to serve is perfect freedom,
through Jesus Christ our Lord. Amen (Alleluia).

(St Augustine)